Decorating Master Class

ELISSA CULLMAN

TRACEY WINN PRUZAN

Decorating Master Class

PRINCIPAL PHOTOGRAPHY BY DURSTON SAYLOR

ABRAMS, NEW YORK

Contents

Introduction

IF THE VERY THOUGHT OF DECORATING YOUR HOME SENDS YOU INTO A PANIC, READ ON AND RELAX. CREATING A BEAUTIFUL, FUNCTIONAL, AND COMFORTABLE ENVIRONMENT IS NOT A SIMPLE OR EASY PROCESS. BUT NEITHER SHOULD IT BE AN OVERWHELMING EXPERIENCE. AT CULLMAN & KRAVIS WE BELIEVE THAT THERE IS NO GREAT SECRET TO DECORATING. IT IS A LOGICAL, RATIONAL PROCESS THAT ANYONE CAN UNDERSTAND AND ADOPT, WHETHER YOU ARE RENOVATING AN EXISTING HOME OR BUILDING A NEW ONE.

THE PURPOSE OF THIS BOOK IS TO DEMYSTIFY THE DECORATING PROCESS—TO DEMONSTRATE THE BASIC PRINCIPLES THAT WE FOLLOW WHEN WE WORK WITH CLIENTS. WE HAVE WRITTEN THE BOOK FOR ANYONE WHO HAS DECIDED TO DECORATE A HOUSE OR AN APARTMENT, WITH OR WITHOUT THE HELP OF A DESIGN PROFESSIONAL. WE HAVE INCLUDED DETAILED INFORMATION ABOUT MATERIALS AND PROCESSES AND PHOTOGRAPHS ILLUSTRATING OUR METHODS AND IDEAS.

OF COURSE, BEHIND ALL THE CAREFUL LOGIC AND THEORY IS INSPIRATION. TRACEY PRUZAN, MY COLLEAGUE OF FOURTEEN YEARS, AND I WILL EXPLAIN MANY OF THE IDEAS THAT MOTIVATE US, AS WELL AS OFFER PRACTICAL SUGGESTIONS ON HOW YOU CAN FIND THE CREATIVE IMPULSE TO DECORATE YOUR OWN HOME.

OPPOSITE:
Where does inspiration come from? Ellie's passion for Americana lights a fire in the living room of her house in Stamford, Connecticut. Over the mantel, a 19th-century portrait by Ammi Phillips is framed by rooster weather vanes and a spongeware bowl and pitcher.

When my partner, the late Hedi Kravis, and I first established Cullman & Kravis more than twenty years ago, we were both amazed at the amount of information we had gathered in our hearts and minds over the years—information about our own lives and about the ways in which we had set up our own homes. I never imagined as I was growing up that I would become a decorator. In fact, my education in decorating was based more on personal life experiences than on any formal training in interior design.

I studied history and art history in college, and I traveled extensively, falling in love with the cultures of Europe and the Far East. But looking back, I can say that there have been several significant influences on my life as a designer. The first is family, beginning with my husband's mother, Louise Cullman, who was a serious collector of early American furniture and Americana when these were not yet fashionable. Years ago, Americans looked to Europe for inspiration, because our homegrown aesthetic carried little value as a source for decoration. Over the years, she introduced me to the bold colors and graphic design of American hooked rugs and quilts, the abstraction of game boards, and the whimsical spirit of weather vanes and pull toys. I became passionate about Americana and co-curated two shows at the Museum of American Folk Art. The first, Andy Warhol's "Folk and Funk," exhibited the Pop artist's remarkably extensive collection.

ABOVE:
Ellie Cullman and
Hedi Kravis

OPPOSITE:
Hedi's extensive Delft collection, grouped and displayed on the mantel and casually arranged on tabletops, brought a wonderful richness of color to her living room in Bedford, New York, c. 1990. The Sultanabad carpet, the Hudson River scene over the mantel, and an American wing chair, all from the 19th century, complete the ambience of this inviting room.

For the second exhibit, "Small Folk: A Celebration of Childhood in America," I coauthored a book with the same title and accompanied the show as it traveled from New York City to St. Louis and then to Japan.

My connection to Japan, which had been forged earlier when my husband and I lived in Tokyo for two years, formed the second pivotal step in the development of my aesthetic vision and education. While my husband was off at work, I would immerse myself in two of the rigorous aesthetic traditions of Japan—tea ceremony and flower arranging. When you spend three hours with a flower instructor arranging just five chrysanthemums, it sharpens your eye! While we were in Japan, the concepts of *kazari*, *wabi sabi*, and *shibui* began to fascinate me. *Kazari* is a philosophy of decoration that calls attention to every surface through embellishment and articulation, whereas *wabi sabi* asks us to look for perfection and beauty in the imperfect and minor details of everyday objects, to find beauty in what is inconspicuous or overlooked, in what is rustic, honest, and simple. The term *shibui* refers to beauty that is sub-dued, unassuming, and refined. Striking a balance between these three concepts is the ultimate goal in my design work.

One of my most profound aesthetic experiences occurred one night when my husband and I received a rare—and most welcome—invitation to an intimate dinner at the home of a lacquer artisan. As we sat on simple tatami mats, his wife served an elaborate ten-course meal, with each dish presented in one of his lacquer vessels, many of them cinnabar-and-black decorated with gold. Sitting in the dimly lit room, basking in the glow of warm sake and delicious food, I was awed by the beauty of the accidental arrangement of the richly colored pieces on the low table and the subtle interplay of light and shadow. A perfect balance was struck between carefully planned ritual and spontaneous effect. It is an ideal that has continued to inspire my work as my firm has grown.

The young people in my office are also endlessly inspiring to me. There are about twenty of them working on our team at any given time, from senior project managers to summer interns, and I could not do what I do without them. Smart and savvy, bursting with energy, they

RIGHT:
Hedi's personal collections were legendary. She felt that tortoiseshell objects matched her warm coloring and amassed a fine collection of pieces like these arranged here on her dressing table.

are constantly asking questions and offering fresh points of view. The lesson is this: I don't work by myself and neither should you. Having a sounding board close at hand, whether friends, family, colleagues, or trusted vendors, will clarify your own ideas and improve your work.

Perhaps the person with the greatest impact on my design life was Hedi Kravis, first my best friend and later my business partner. Our collaboration began somewhat serendipitously in 1984. Hedi and I had written a screenplay about an ambitious 1980s couple whose marriage is wrecked by an obsession to possess all the material goods that a high-living household should have. We presented the screenplay, called *All of the Trappings*, to a film producer friend, Stanley Jaffe. Much to our surprise, he determined that we had absolutely no talent for screenwriting. He did, however, love the way we described the characters' homes in the screenplay and suggested that our real skills might lie in decorating rather than in the film business. Jaffe became our first client when he commissioned us on the spot to decorate his Park Avenue apartment—and thus Cullman & Kravis was born.

Hedi and I worked together for thirteen years before she died in 1997. She was gorgeous and glamorous, with impeccable taste, keen attention to detail, and an uncanny ability to divine the coming styles. Hedi was also a natural-born collector and an instinctive interior designer. She was the first to have an all-white apartment, designed to set off a growing collection of antique tortoiseshell objects, which she always believed was the ideal complement to her own olive complexion and gold-flecked green eyes. By the early 1980s, her focus shifted from eclectic modern to American and English eighteenth- and nineteenth-century furniture—"high style" in her New York apartment and "high country" in her Bedford house. Friends were dazzled by the layers of her collections, from Dutch Delft and period brass to faux bamboo and painted furniture. One very special room was the dining room. Double-glazed in cornflower blue, the space incorporated eight convex mirrors and an extraordinary set of dining-room chairs with *verre églomisé* backs, each one depicting a different country scene. The room "twinkled," to use Hedi's word, making the objects (as well as the guests) look luminous.

LEFT:
Hedi's dining room was all about "twinkle." The walls, covered with a lively double-glazed cornflower blue, are outlined in a gold edge. The Regency chairs boast *églomisé* (reverse painting on glass) back splats, and a grouping of bull's-eye mirrors reflects the ambient glow. Just as jewelry adds sparkle to a woman's appearance, shiny surfaces such as the brass sconces, candlesticks, and andirons add sparkle to a room.

Because Ellie wanted a screened-in porch that she could enjoy year-round, architect John B. Murray came up with an ingenious solution. In the winter months, the triple-hung windows, which are glazed with insulated glass, transform the space into a cozy sunroom. In the warmer months, the same windows easily slide into an overhead pocket, revealing screens behind. Since one of Ellie's greatest passions is folk art, she has filled the room with cigar-store Indians, weather vanes, and game boards.

The Cullman & Kravis approach has evolved with time, as we have grown into a midsize Madison Avenue firm with clients and installations all over the United States. But our mantra, which crystallized early on, has stayed constant, and that is: Never draw a line between architecture and decoration—they must work in tandem, unquestionably. We collaborate very closely with architects on all of our projects, ensuring that the architecture is in harmony with the decorating. As we like to say, architecture comes first, and there is no successful decoration without good "bones."

We have also never wavered from our belief that good decorating has to be more than creating something pretty. "Pretty" is just not interesting enough, because a magnificent space that does not perform its function is a failure. But a space that responds solely to the burdens of practicality is a wasted opportunity. A successfully decorated room strikes a fine balance between aesthetics and the day-to-day demands of modern life.

Before we embark on any project, we go to great lengths to understand our client's goals and aspirations. An essential first step is to establish the scope of the project—the extent of the work from the floor plans to construction, purchasing, and installation—as well as a realistic idea of the budget. If you cannot complete a project all at once because you do not have the time or the money, you can save yourself a great deal of trouble by figuring out your entire wish list before getting started. If the overall concept is clear, you can successfully implement the different pieces of the project as your budget and schedule allow. In the end, the result of your planning will be better designed spaces that flow together and relate more successfully to each other.

It is true that decorating is a glamorous pursuit. But it also generates mounds of paperwork and entails coordinating deliveries and supervising complex installations. Every day we interact with a large cast of vendors, colleagues, and clients. Still, from the mundane to the sublime, I am passionate about the work I do to the point of obsession, whether it is picking the right trim, experimenting with a new decorative paint technique, or discovering a new antiques dealer.

The culmination of all our effort comes after we have plumped the last pillow, dressed the last curtain, and filled the last empty frame. We pop open Champagne to toast and celebrate. Our reward is a happy client and a sophisticated interior that is useful, functional, beautiful, and classic. The Cullman & Kravis style is timeless; we do not decorate according to what is merely fashionable in home design. Our point of view is uniquely American, we feel, in that is driven by concerns about function and aesthetics alike. To us, American design has purity and is never precious. And that is what we want for our clients—real homes for real people.

Ellie Cullman

Chapter 1: Starting Out

OVER THE YEARS, WE HAVE ENCOUNTERED MANY MISCONCEPTIONS ABOUT DECORATING. A COMMON ONE IS THAT THE DECORATOR IS ALL KNOWING AND CAN PROCLAIM SOMETHING LIKE "I SEE PINK!" AS SOON AS HE OR SHE WALKS INTO A ROOM. BUT DECORATORS HAVE TO DO A LOT OF PRELIMINARY WORK BEFORE THEY CAN "SEE" ANYTHING. ANOTHER FALLACY IS THAT YOU CAN GET AWAY WITH DOING A CURSORY JOB BECAUSE "YOU CAN ALWAYS MAKE CHANGES LATER." THIS IS NEVER A SUCCESSFUL APPROACH. EVEN IF YOU CANNOT IMPLEMENT AT ONCE EVERYTHING YOU ULTIMATELY WANT TO DO, TRY TO FIGURE OUT THE BIG PICTURE AT THE OUTSET, BECAUSE IT WILL BE MUCH EASIER TO MAKE SENSIBLE DECISIONS LATER IF YOU HAVE PLANNED AHEAD.

NOW THAT WE HAVE CLEARED UP THOSE TWO MYTHS, HOW, EXACTLY, *DOES* ONE GET STARTED WITH A DECORATING PROJECT? IN A NUTSHELL, IT INVOLVES A BIT OF EDUCATION, LOGIC, AND SELF-EVALUATION.

OPPOSITE:
Because the dining room is often the least used room in a house, how do you make it do double duty? Use it as a library. Line the walls with books, use a cheerful check fabric on the chairs, and allow for extra light. Disks in the dining tabletop pop out to reveal outlets to plug in reading lamps. (Claus Rademacher, architect)

EDUCATE YOURSELF

You can develop your personal vision by browsing through design books and magazines, and by visiting museums, shops, auctions, and flea markets. Travel is also endlessly inspiring and educational. Record your findings by making notes, taking photographs, and collecting pictures. File your ideas, photos, and drawings in a notebook, a binder, or simple folders to create a personal design reference library. Maintaining your library is very important, because even something as seemingly inconsequential as a piece of colored glass can be the catalyst for a great room or a design motif. Revisit and revise your library often. You may be surprised to find that what you like—and do not like, which is equally important—may be different than what you initially thought. Over time, your vocabulary of preferred styles, shapes, and colors will emerge, and you will soon develop an "eye" for design.

ASSESS YOUR NEEDS

Once you begin to sense your own style, it is time to think critically about what makes a room work. To fully understand how you live in your home, examine how you live now as opposed to how you want to live after the work is done. Take careful stock of your possessions and determine what you plan to keep versus what you hope to replace. Lastly, you must decide if your project requires an architect, a decorator, or a builder/contractor. Here is how we do it.

Step 1: Understand Your Functional Requirements

Asking our clients the questions below is one of the first steps in our process, because it helps us to prioritize the practical needs of the home. Choose the topics that apply to your particular project, and your own answers will help you design successful, usable spaces.

RIGHT:
Ellie's dining room in Stamford strikes a patriotic red, white, and blue theme, in keeping with her passion for Americana. If you include what you love in your décor, you will add history and depth to every room.

OPPOSITE:
This Manhattan library doubles as a home office—with a 14-foot desktop and a computer in plain sight. Four club chairs, placed in an X formation with a round coffee table in the center, are particularly conducive to conversation.

Occupants. How many people live here? Are they permanent or occasional residents? Are there any children, elderly parents, or other people with special needs? Ages, relationships, and abilities will help determine the size and location of bedrooms and bathrooms.

Type of residence. Is this a primary residence or a second home? A year-round house will have different climate-control requirements than a summer or a winter residence. A weekend house will have storage and other needs that are different from those of the primary house.

Kitchen. Do you like to cook? Do you want a professional-style kitchen? Do you want enough room so that family and friends can hang out or do homework while you cook? Are there specific brands or pieces of equipment you prefer? Do you need a lot of space to store food, kitchen utensils, and cooking equipment, as well as other supplies for cleaning, first aid, garbage, and more?

General dining. What are your informal and formal dining needs? Where do you most commonly dine with your family? With friends and guests? If you prefer informal family meals in the kitchen, we might recommend a breakfast nook and a casual table for dining rather than a formal dining room.

Entertaining. Do you entertain? How frequently? Is your style formal or casual? How many people do you generally host (minimum? maximum?)? Try to assess accurately and honestly your capacity and willingness to entertain, because the answers will affect the layouts of your kitchen, living room, and dining room. For example, if you find yourself regularly inviting fourteen people for cocktails and dinner, your rooms should be able to accommodate everyone sitting together for cocktails and then sitting down at the table for dinner. Otherwise, you will need to set up a buffet on these occasions. Also, if you entertain a

lot, you may want additional, convenient storage spaces for china, linens, and even guests' coats. If you entertain mostly on holidays, your dining room should be big enough to allow you to expand your table to seat extra people. Consider, too, whether you use caterers for large events and what additional setup or storage space might be useful.

Baths. How many bathrooms do you need? Who will use them? How many individual bathrooms will be required? How many bathrooms will be shared? Does anyone with special needs require a walk-in shower or other equipment? Are there special features or equipment you desire, such as grab bars, sauna, whirlpool, extra outlets in the cabinetry for shaving and blow dryers, extra lighting, or extra ventilation? Do not forget child-friendly storage and faucets.

Home office. Will anyone be working at home? What electrical equipment is needed—such as a printer, a fax machine, a copier—and where

should these pieces be located or stored within the room? What about increased electrical sources or Internet access? Where in your home will it make the most sense to place a home office—near or far from activity centers, such as the family room or the children's bedrooms and playroom?

Media/technology. Where will you and your family use computers and televisions? How many do you need? How many people will watch television at one time? Beyond a home office, where do you need Internet access? Given our modern reliance on the Internet, you may want to wire each room for access or provide for a wireless network when you are renovating rather than having to retrofit the house later on.

Guests. Do you frequently have overnight guests? Where would you like their rooms in relation to the rest of your family? Can you accommodate a guest bathroom?

Storage. What are your general storage requirements? Room by room, consider what you will need to keep in open, accessible storage as opposed to what can be kept in closed cabinets, drawers, or closets. Does your family participate in sports, and do you have a lot of athletic equipment to stow away? There are many clever storage and space-saving solutions for athletic equipment. Do you have other hobbies that require specialized storage or space, as in a craft or sewing room?

Collections. Do you need to display your collections in some way? Do your collections require specialized lighting or climate control?

Additional work space. Do you have a housekeeper, a nanny, or an office assistant who works in your home? Consider their needs for work space and privacy.

Pets. Do you have pets? Do your pets need direct access to a yard through a door or mudroom? If you have a dog and a cat, where will you feed them? Where will you put such items as litter boxes?

Utility rooms. Where do you want to put your laundry room? (Upstairs is often more convenient than the first floor or basement.) Do you generate enough laundry to require multiple washing machines? Make sure you factor in the space to set up an ironing board, to air-dry fine washables, and to hand wash delicate garments. Do you keep a garden? A mudroom with a deep sink for cut flowers and shelves for vase and equipment storage is a nice luxury if you have the space.

"There is always a burst of creativity, but there is no magic wand that makes it all come together."

OPPOSITE:
The greatest luxury is the tranquility of a wide-open space. The entrance hall of this East Hampton home, decorated in muted tones of sand and sea, brings the limestone floor from the outside in, making a smooth transition from outdoors to indoors. (Andrew Pollock, architect)

LEFT:
Your eyes are like a camera to the world, so why not focus on the view while you bathe? This multitasking master bath has it all; you can watch television and take phone calls while you wash up. The natural stone and materials emphasize the sense of place in this Vail penthouse. (Gordon Pierce, architect)

Step 2: Inventory Your Possessions

Spend some time assessing what you have, where everything should go, and what you may need or wish to buy in the future. We cannot stress enough the importance of making a careful and accurate inventory of all of your possessions. A primary inventory should include photographs by room of all furniture, objects, and works of art, with dimensions carefully noted. Make a secondary list that includes linens, dishware, and clothing to which you can refer as you plan for sufficient and appropriate storage in the final design of your project. To organize your inventory, set up binders with labeled subject dividers for each room and a separate piece of paper with the photo, the measurements, and other pertinent information for every item.

Refer to your inventory when you draw floor plans, and use it to keep track of what you have if your belongings are in storage during construction. By keeping it accurate and up to date, you will have an instant record for your insurance company as well.

Step 3: Work with Your Project Team

You may, of course, decorate your own home, and books like this can help. However, on complex projects, we always recommend teaming up with industry professionals, such as architects, general contractors, or specific subcontractors, such as plumbers, electricians, cabinetmakers, specialist painters, upholsterers, kitchen experts, art consultants, a landscape architect, and others, to get the job done efficiently. Collaborating with these professionals will help you reach your goals, avoid costly mistakes, and free up your time for other things. One further note: If you are considering the purchase of a new home, you may find it useful to take an architect and a decorator with you to review the potential space. Before you make a commitment, they will be able to determine what they can achieve and whether that will match your goals.

"Just as important as knowing your likes and dislikes is knowing what you need."

OPPOSITE:
If you love to travel or entertain, you know that there is never a good space to pack a bag, nor are there enough extra beds for guests. An oversize window seat in Ellie's Connecticut dressing room adds an extra surface for either activity.

LEFT:
An architect can often capture extra space you didn't know you had. Here bookcase niches were carved under the eaves of the master bedroom of this country house. A dormer window adds a source of light. (Ira Grandberg, architect)

THE ARCHITECT. A qualified, licensed architect is the only person who can ensure that the structural and stylistic details of your home will be correct and consistent and who can obtain necessary building permits. Even if you are considering a relatively minor renovation, such as a new guest bath, an architect can be invaluable in suggesting ideas, preparing floor plans and elevation drawings, and helping supervise the contractor.

THE DECORATOR. We always recommend that the architect and interior designer be hired at the same time. If you begin construction or renovation without floor plans and without figuring out accurate furniture placement, you run the risk of making costly mistakes. A responsible interior decorator provides critical input at all stages of construction and can be the key to the success of your project.

THE CONTRACTOR. Your architect and your decorator will have a list of contractors with whom they have successfully collaborated in the past, or you may have your own list of good contractors who have been recommended to you. Choose three contractors and give them the plans on which they can base cost estimates. Three bids should give you a realistic sense of the range of costs, and a meeting with each contractor should give you an idea of the personalities involved.

Do not award your contract just on the basis of the lowest bid. Quality of construction is critical, but the contractor-client relationship is important, too. Will the contractor come back to fix things after the job is completed? Do you like the contractor as a person? This may seem obvious, but it is important that you feel you can trust and work agreeably with the contractor before you become involved. Timing is also

"Clients are often instantly turned off by a place because of the existing décor or condition. It is helpful to take a designer and architect to a site before you decide whether or not to buy it. A professional team will be able to tell immediately what can be achieved and whether that will match their client's goals."

RIGHT:
Space is usually at a premium in a city apartment. Here the library doubles as a study and television room. The plasma screen pops up from a hidden slot in the bookcase but is out of sight for formal entertaining. (John B. Murray, architect)

OPPOSITE:
The study walls are clad in tongue-and-groove paneling, and the wood has been limed to bring out the grain. The painting above the fireplace conceals a plasma television and can be raised by the motorized track on which it is hung. You can do this only if your ceiling is high enough to accommodate the painting when it is raised. (Botticelli and Pohl, architects)

important. Will the contractor propose a schedule that works for you? Ask your contractor to discuss price changes with you. If he quotes a price for material, for example, but you do not buy the material for six months, what happens if the price goes up? He will undoubtedly pass this increase on to you, but you should have a discussion and a clear understanding about these possibilities before you begin. Remember that you will inevitably make some changes and that there will be change orders—signed agreements for implementing a change—and extra costs involved in doing so. The most important piece of advice is that you enter this (like all other significant relationships!) with your eyes wide open.

How to Use This Book

We approach each of our projects in a linear way. We follow steps that begin with simple ideas translated into floor plans. We select hard and soft materials, place our orders, and conclude, after much hard work, with the installation. We have written this book to reflect the same logical steps that we follow, even though we always review and revise earlier decisions as the project evolves. Similarly, you should read the chapters of this book in sequence but be prepared to move back and forth between chapters as you review your decisions, and perhaps change your mind about different aspects of your own project goals.

In the chapters that follow, we explain the thinking behind all the choices you will face in your construction or renovation projects, and we analyze our solutions through case studies of actual spaces Cullman & Kravis has decorated. You will see photographs of completed rooms, as well as photographs of specific elements, such as wall surfaces and pillows. Floor plans, elevation drawings, and renderings are the tools of our trade, and we have included them here as well. Occasional sidebars appear in each chapter to introduce some of our signature concepts ("The C&K Way"), to call out important information ("Do You Know?"), and to offer advice on some universal decorating issues ("Solutions"). At the end of the book, we provide a guide to creating and maintaining your own project books, an important Cullman & Kravis tool for any project, and a list of books that we have found both useful and inspiring.

CASE STUDY:

The owners of this large master bedroom wanted to relax or watch television, but not only from the bed. This problem was solved by the cabinet at the foot of the bed, which houses a plasma television and can rotate 360 degrees, to be seen from the sofa, the desk (not visible), and, of course, the king-size bed. (Jacquelyn Robertson, architect)

Chapter 2: The Floor Plan

ALL DECORATING PROJECTS, NO MATTER HOW LARGE OR SMALL, SHOULD BEGIN WITH A CAREFUL STUDY OF THE FLOOR PLANS. THINK OF THEM AS THE STRUCTURAL FRAMEWORKS OF YOUR ROOMS.

AT ITS MOST BASIC, A FLOOR PLAN IS A TWO-DIMENSIONAL DRAWING THAT INDICATES THE SPATIAL ARRANGEMENT OF A ROOM. THE KEY TO THE FLOOR PLAN IS THAT IT IS DRAWN TO SCALE—A GRAPHIC REPRESENTATION OF THE ACTUAL SIZE OF SPACES AND OBJECTS. A DRAWING IN ½-INCH SCALE MEANS THAT ½ INCH ON PAPER EQUALS 1 FOOT IN REALITY. IN OTHER WORDS, AN 8-FOOT SOFA WOULD BE 4 INCHES LONG ON PAPER. THE FLOOR PLAN ALLOWS A DESIGNER TO ARRANGE AND STUDY THE CONTENTS OF THE ROOM TO SEE HOW THINGS RELATE TO EACH OTHER, IN ORDER TO ACHIEVE THE BEST POSSIBLE ROOM LAYOUT. IT ALSO HELPS THE DESIGNER SELECT NEW PIECES IN THE MOST APPROPRIATE SHAPES AND SIZES. HOWEVER, THE SHAPES ON THE FLOOR PLAN ARE FAR MORE THAN SIMPLE GEOMETRY. THEY ALSO REFLECT CAREFULLY MADE CHOICES ABOUT MATERIALS, SIZES, COLOR DISTRIBUTION, AND TRAFFIC FLOW.

OPPOSITE:
If you look at a room as just a floor plan, you don't see the subtle differences between the shapes in a room. The only way to make correct choices is to have a vision of the room as a whole, but this awareness comes with trial and error, time and practice. The area rug by Elizabeth Eakins, called "Medallions and Crosses," was made large enough to hold all the furniture comfortably and to allow the colorful rug border to be seen around the perimeter of the seating area. Most of the furniture pieces are in pairs. To relieve the symmetry, the chairs at the bottom of the frame are unmatched in shape, scale, and upholstery fabric. (David Beckwith, architect)

The basic floor plan of this living room would indicate the careful placement of furniture, including a pair of chairs and a pair of consoles, with lamps flanking the fireplace. Only a fully rendered plan would show the subtleties of the beige and red palette, which is created by the mix of solid, check, and curvilinear patterns on the fabrics and in the rug. Not visible in the plan are the high ceiling and dramatic double-height windows that give this room its real character, but these would be evident in elevation drawings. (Claus Rademacher, architect)

RIGHT BOTTOM:
To create symmetry in this Manhattan dining room, architect Elliot Rosenblum added the faux doorway seen at the left in this picture.

OPPOSITE:
Every hallway and landing offer an opportunity to tell a story with materials, paint, light, accessories, and works of art. Consider these spaces as you would any other room on your floor plan. Make an effort to balance closed and open forms and light and dark materials, such as those seen in this beach-house landing on an island in South Carolina. A shell-framed mirror, scattered coral, and photographs of windsurfers reflect the house's setting. Don't forget that a mirror at the end of a long vista reflects light and makes the journey down the hall a more pleasant experience. (Mark Finlay, architect)

Drawing Your Floor Plan

Drawing a floor plan is not very complicated, but drawing an accurate one is not as simple as it looks. You may find it helpful to draw a preliminary plan on which you can work out some of your ideas. However, we suggest asking an architect or an interior designer to draw the final floor plan, which will be used to convey information to the contractor and subcontractors. There are many books, computer programs, and templates available that will help you draw a plan. But drawing is the easy part. Whether you draw your own, or use someone else's plan, you will have to think like a designer in order to make sense of what you are seeing and to ensure that your rooms have a rhythm, with objects that relate to one another.

We make multiple floor plans for each room, because there are many ways to analyze a room and many choices that must be made to achieve a plan that will meet your goals. Remember that you will need to be flexible, creative, and sensitive to all the possibilities as well as to the limitations of your home to see what works—and what doesn't! Redrawing your floor plan is an inexpensive way to experiment with your design concepts before you execute an expensive idea that may turn out to be a mistake.

Being an interior designer involves looking at floor-plan options from different points of view. The goal is to understand the impact that your decisions will have on the way you live (think back to the self-analysis questionnaire in Chapter 1). In the end, the floor plan will be your guide to help you identify what you really want from each room and a tool that will help you attain that goal.

The Elements of a Floor Plan

For a full house renovation, you will need an overall plan of the entire building, plus individual floor plans for every room. Each room's plan should include the outline of the room, the location of architectural elements (walls, doors, windows, fireplaces, and so on), and representations of major furniture pieces and rugs. A more detailed floor plan might illustrate curtains, incidental tables and chairs, loose pillows, and light fixtures. Your floor plan should take into account what you already own and what you wish to add, indicating optimal sizes for the missing pieces. Eventually, the floor plan may include renderings of the materials you have chosen (stone, wood, carpet, fabrics), and even notations on specific colors and designs.

The Rhythms of Rooms, the Relationships of Objects

It is important to understand the implications of the placement of doors and windows. Is there architectural symmetry in the room that you can enhance with your choices of furniture, such as pairs of chairs or tables? Alternatively, if you add any new architectural elements, think how they will impact the room. Will a sofa still fit if you add a door on one wall? If you want French doors, be sure that you will be able to open them without hitting pieces of furniture.

The floor plan will make a room's inherent architectural issues apparent at a glance. Some existing spaces are complicated and do not have a logical, natural flow to them. There may be a lack of symmetry or a clumsy juxtaposition of a door or window. As you review the floor plan, confer with your architect to address and correct these problems in the early stages of the project. To balance an offset door, for example, we have often made surface adjustments, such as creating a fake door that can provide symmetry and create a better view from one room to another. We have also enlarged a doorway to create a centered, double-wide opening, which gives greater visual and physical access to the next room. Even if you are not renovating or building, being aware of these types of issues can help you understand why your room is not working or the possibilities for improving your existing space.

Is there enough room for your furniture—including treasured existing pieces, as well as proposed purchases—along the walls, below the windows, and between the doors? Look at the overall size of each room to evaluate whether it can hold the appropriate furniture: standard pieces such as a bed and two night tables in the bedrooms; a dining table and chairs with a storage piece, such as a sideboard in the dining room, and so on.

To really understand the nuances of furniture pieces, reexamine the plan in terms of groups: soft pieces (upholstered) and hard (wood, metal, or glass); open forms (exposed furniture legs) and closed (furniture legs concealed behind skirts); airy volumes (table) and solid (chest of drawers); low shapes (coffee table) and high (bookcase). This awareness comes with time and practice.

Do your rooms have rhythm, with objects that relate to one another? Vary the forms and materials throughout the room as you begin to think ahead and imagine what the room will look like. For example, if you have placed two matched sofas in a living room along with two club chairs, plan to have some degree of variation, but not so much as to make you dizzy. If the sofas match each other both in shape and upholstery, their fabric covering should be different from that of the club chairs. If one of the chairs is upholstered and the other is a wooden frame with an upholstered seat, you would have one open form and one closed form, and that would make the arrangement less static but still classic. (There will be more about upholstery selection in Chapter 6.) If you want a matching pair of upholstered club chairs, complement them with a wood-framed chair as a third seat to add variety of form and texture.

If your coffee table is very open—made of glass and brass—one end table might be a small wooden chest and the other a round pedestal table. End tables don't have to match, but you will do your room a favor if they are the same height so that a matched pair of table lamps upon them will be the same height, too. If all your furniture shapes look like rectangles, try to add some softness in the form of a chair with a curved back, a round side table, a round ottoman under the piano, or a pair of demilune console tables somewhere in the room.

Deciding how to distribute your furniture forms on paper before you start shopping for new pieces is the best way to avoid costly mistakes.

"Negative space can be a very positive element in design."

RIGHT:
The elevation of the living-room wall in this Manhattan pied-à-terre confirmed that the clients' abstract pen drawings by Alighiero Boetti could fit and be centered on the wall with the primary sofa.

BOTTOM RIGHT:
An elevation drawing of the south wall of the living room above.

OPPOSITE:
The fireplace in this Vail penthouse is fashioned from river rocks collected in the area. (Gordon Pierce, architect)

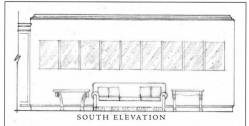

SOUTH ELEVATION

Use the floor plan to narrow your focus as you make selections and purchases. Wherever we are—in the office, out shopping with a client, meeting with vendors—we always refer to the floor plan for guidance. We give a copy of the plan to our clients to use while they are shopping on their own for art or antiques, and we fax the plan to special dealers for suggestions of antiques to fit our floor plan.

Elevation Drawings: The Partners of Your Floor Plan

Make an effort to envision the geometric shapes on the floor plan as more than simple outlines. To determine the exact nature of the furniture forms in your room, you should consider those forms in both plan and elevation. Drawn to scale like a floor plan, an elevation is a line drawing of a wall and the furniture in front of it. You can think of an elevation drawing as a diorama. The floor plan shows us the big picture of a room seen from above, but the elevations let us see the details as if we were actually in the room. Each piece of furniture planned for a room must be drawn in elevation before we start our search for new pieces, or we may end up making the wrong selections. Elevations are just as important as floor plans. Most clients lack the capacity or training to execute elevations on their own, and will need help from an architect or decorator.

Allow for Improvement and Evolution

In addition to current problems you may wish to fix, you should also review your floor plans with future flexibility in mind. The basic footprint of your room can remain the same. But be sure to consider how you can convert the room easily as your needs change. For example, certain rooms need to adapt occasionally to special occasions. For entertaining a large party, a dining room should be able to accommodate an expanded table and additional seating. Other rooms, such as a baby's room, need to evolve to serve different functions over time as the child grows.

The C&K Way: Envisioning a Floor Plan in 3-D

ONCE YOU THINK YOU MAY HAVE HIT UPON THE IDEAL FLOOR PLAN, IT IS TIME TO EVALUATE YOUR TWO-DIMENSIONAL DREAMS IN ORDER TO ENVISION YOUR ULTIMATE THREE-DIMENSIONAL REALITY. BUT IT CAN BE REALLY HARD TO MAKE A DECISION JUST BY LOOKING AT THE FLOOR PLAN ON PAPER. IT IS AN ENTIRELY DIFFERENT EXPERIENCE TO VIEW A ROOM IN THREE DIMENSIONS THAN IT IS TO SEE A FLAT PLAN ON PAPER. WHEN WE ARE WORKING ON LOCAL PROJECTS IN NEW YORK CITY, WE OFTEN HAVE THE LUXURY OF "TRYING OUT" UPHOLSTERED PIECES AND ANTIQUE FURNITURE IN THE ACTUAL ROOM BEFORE WE MAKE A PURCHASE. HOWEVER, THAT IS NOT THE CASE WHEN WE HAVE AN OUT-OF-TOWN PROJECT OR ONE THAT INVOLVES CONSTRUCTION FROM THE GROUND UP. IT IS IMPRACTICAL AND SOMETIMES IMPOSSIBLE TO CREATE AN ACTUAL LIFE-SIZE MOCKUP OF THE ROOM TO CHOOSE THE BEST FLOOR PLAN. SO, THE MOST EFFECTIVE APPROACH TO UNDERSTANDING FLOOR PLANS IS TO TRAIN YOUR EYE BY NOTICING FURNITURE LAYOUTS WHEREVER YOU GO, ANALYZING WHAT WORKS AND WHAT DOESN'T. TAKE MENTAL AND WRITTEN NOTES OF THE RELATIVE SIZES OF SOFAS, CHAIRS, AND TABLES. YOU CAN ALSO TAKE PHOTOGRAPHS OF PLEASING FURNITURE ARRANGEMENTS YOU COME ACROSS AND KEEP THEM FOR REFERENCE.

The C&K Way: The Fireplace as Your Compass

NOT EVERY ROOM WILL HAVE A FIREPLACE. BUT IF YOURS DOES, THE EASIEST WAY TO DETERMINE WHAT WILL GO WHERE ON YOUR FLOOR PLAN IS TO CONSIDER THE ELEVATION OF THE FIREPLACE WALL, BECAUSE THAT IS WHERE YOU WILL FIND THE LEAST AMOUNT OF "FORM FLEXIBILITY." THE FIREPLACE IS A GIVEN—MEANING THAT WE CANNOT CHANGE ITS SIZE OR SHAPE.

IN A LIVING ROOM, CASE PIECES (SUCH AS CHESTS, CREDENZAS, BOOKCASES, OR SECRETARY DESKS) SHOULD NOT FLANK THE FIREPLACE, BECAUSE TWO SOLID MASSES COMBINED WITH THE FIREPLACE WOULD RESULT IN THREE DARK FORMS OF ABOUT THE SAME SHAPE ALL LINED UP ON A MAJOR WALL. IT WOULD BE BETTER TO PLACE OPEN FORMS, SUCH AS CONSOLES, OPEN PARSONS AND CARD TABLES, AND SMALL ÉTAGÉRES, ON EITHER SIDE OF A FIREPLACE.

IF YOU ARE ADDING A NEW FIREPLACE TO YOUR HOME, HERE ARE SOME GUIDELINES FOR DETERMINING THE DIMENSIONS OF A MANTEL AND FIREPLACE OPENING:

*WIDTH. IN EARLY HOUSE DESIGN, CHIMNEYS WERE BUILT ON THE OUTSIDE OF THE HOUSE. BY THE 1780S, CHIMNEYS WERE BUILT ON THE INSIDE, FORMING A "BUMP" WHERE THE CHIMNEY PROJECTED INTO THE ROOM AND CREATING AN ATTRACTIVE SPOT FOR A PICTURE ABOVE THE MANTEL. HISTORICALLY, THE MANTEL SHELF LINED UP TO THE EDGE OF THE BUMP. BUT WE PREFER TO HAVE

RIGHT:
The sculptural form of the Regency armchair in the foreground is an effective counterpoint to the mass of the upholstered sofa. Some of the furniture forms are full and upholstered, whereas others are light and airy with exposed wooden arms and legs.

SOME SPACE—ABOUT 4 TO 6 INCHES ON EITHER SIDE OF THE EDGE OF THE SHELF. IF YOU PUT SCONCES OVER THE MANTEL, THE EXTRA SPACE LETS THEM BREATHE.

*HEIGHT. A GENERAL RULE OF THUMB TO DETERMINE THE PROPER HEIGHT OF THE MANTEL IS TO TAKE THE CEILING HEIGHT, DIVIDE IT IN HALF, AND THEN PLACE THE SHELF ABOVE THAT CENTERLINE. FOR INSTANCE, IF YOUR CEILING HEIGHT IS 9 FEET, THEN 4 ½ FEET IS THE CENTERLINE. AN IDEAL MANTEL HEIGHT WOULD FALL SOMEWHERE BETWEEN 5 AND 6 FEET IN HEIGHT.

*SIZE OF OPENING. BE AWARE THAT CITIES AND STATES HAVE DIFFERENT SAFETY CODES FOR FIREPLACES, SO FIND OUT WHAT THE FIRE CODE IN YOUR AREA IS FOR THE SURROUND AND THE HEARTHSTONE. THEY MUST BE MADE OF NONFLAMMABLE MATERIAL, USUALLY A STONE SUCH AS SLATE OR MARBLE. IN MOST CASES, YOU WILL NEED AT LEAST 8 INCHES OF NONFLAMMABLE MATERIAL ON THE SIDES AND 10 INCHES ON TOP. IF YOUR MANTEL IS STONE, THE 10 INCHES CAN INCLUDE THE HEIGHT OF THE MANTEL. IF YOUR MANTEL IS WOOD, THE BOTTOM OF THE MANTEL STARTS AT THE 10-INCH LINE, THUS GIVING YOU A HIGHER OVERALL MANTEL SHELF. ALSO, FIND OUT IF YOU ARE REQUIRED TO HAVE A RAISED OR A FLUSH HEARTH. WE PREFER A FLUSH HEARTH BECAUSE OF ITS CLEAN FINISH. BUT IF YOU HAVE A SMALL MANTEL, A RAISED HEARTH WILL ADD SOME HEIGHT AND MAY HELP KEEP CHILDREN AND DOGS AWAY FROM THE FIREPLACE.

*DEPTH OF OPENING. THE DEPTH OF YOUR HEARTHSTONE IS BASED ON THE BUILDING CODE IN YOUR AREA. BUT THE WIDTH SHOULD EXTEND TO THE OUTSIDE OF THE PILLARS, OR LEGS, ALSO CALLED THE PLINTH.

*SCONCES. TO PLACE SCONCES CORRECTLY OVER THE MANTEL, LINE UP THE CENTER OF EACH SCONCE WITH THE CENTERLINE OF THE PLINTH BLOCK ON THE MANTEL. THE HEIGHT SHOULD BE ABOUT 15 TO 18 INCHES OVER THE TOP OF THE MANTEL, DEPENDING, OF COURSE, ON THE HEIGHT OF THE MANTEL. WHEN NOT SET OVER A MANTEL, MOST SCONCES SHOULD BE HUNG ABOUT 5 FEET 6 INCHES ABOVE THE FINISHED FLOOR (AFF).

*TELEVISION. IF A FLAT-SCREEN TELEVISION IS TO BE MOUNTED ABOVE THE MANTEL AT A COMFORTABLE HEIGHT, THE OPENING FOR THE TELEVISION SHOULD START ABOUT 4 INCHES ABOVE THE MANTEL SHELF. SINCE YOU DON'T WANT TO WATCH A TELEVISION THAT IS TOO HIGH UP ON THE WALL, IT MIGHT BE BETTER TO USE A STONE MANTEL SO THAT THE SURROUND IS LESS AND THE TELEVISION IS LOWER.

*ANDIRONS. THESE SHOULD FILL ABOUT TWO-THIRDS OF THE HEIGHT OF THE OPENING OF THE FIREPLACE.

*FIRE SCREENS. THERE ARE MANY VARIETIES OF FIRE SCREENS, BUT OUR FAVORITE IS CALLED A "SPARK GUARD," WHICH HAS A STATIONARY CURB, SLOTS CUT OUT FOR THE ANDIRONS, AND A DRAWSTRING CURTAIN.

LEFT:
Mantels can be new or old. An early 19th-century American pine mantel from the Delaware Valley is the focal point of this living room. A tall mantel—this one is 58 inches high—in a room with a low ceiling makes the ceiling appear higher.

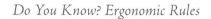

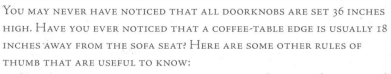

Do You Know? Ergonomic Rules

You may never have noticed that all doorknobs are set 36 inches high. Have you ever noticed that a coffee-table edge is usually 18 inches away from the sofa seat? Here are some other rules of thumb that are useful to know:

Standard table heights include the desk (29 inches), counter (36 inches), and bar (42 inches). The height of a chair or a stool should correspond to the height of the table it accompanies and be at least 10 to 12 inches lower.

Living room. Upholstered chairs and sofas should be at least 36 inches deep from the edge of the seat cushion to the outside back, and the sofa cushion at the back should be at least 18 inches high. There should be at least 3 inches between the sofa and the end tables of each side. A modern end table is usually 2 feet high, but antiques are often 27 to 29 inches in height. Most coffee tables are 18 inches high.

Dining room. The dining table can be 28 to 30 inches high, and standard chairs are 18 inches high. The apron (underside) of a dining table, however, should not be lower than 26 inches, for the comfort of the diner. There should be a minimum of 36 inches around a table for passage; chairs should be at least 18 inches wide. A rug under a dining table should allow you to comfortably pull out a chair without pulling the edge of the rug.

Library. Bookcases should be 12 to 15 inches deep. A desk should be at least 2 feet deep and 29 inches high.

Bedroom. A headboard should be at least 24 to 27 inches higher than the mattress height.

Television. The optimal viewing distance depends on the size of the television set. A general rule for the television viewing distance, based on guidelines developed by the Society of Motion Pictures and Television Engineers, is that the viewing distance between you and your big-screen television should be no closer than about twice the screen width and no farther away than five times the width. This rule of thumb does not necessarily represent the ideal home theater viewing distance but indicates the optimal limits. For a 30-inch screen, the optimal viewing distance is about 6 feet away; with a 65-inch screen, the set should be about 13 ½ feet away.

"Designing an interior is like making a movie. You start with a floor plan—a script—and then the project is developed with the collaboration of many professionals and realized with careful editing."

Opposite:
This billiard room includes a bar and an informal sitting area. Because the beach view is paramount, the furniture is not centered on the fireplace, as would usually be the case in such a room. (Mark Finlay, architect)

ABOVE LEFT:
Sometimes mirrors don't reflect natural light or a great view. Here a 1974 Bill Eggleston photo of a bathroom is poised against a 17th-century Pilgrim chest and a 17th-century Dutch marquetry cushion mirror.

ABOVE RIGHT:
You can never have too much of a good thing. Ellie hung three mirrors in her dining room: the Regency convex mirror, which reflects one of a pair of oval Adam mirrors on the opposite wall, enhances both the natural and the artificial light of this formal room.

Make Sure You Have a Mirror

THE RENOWNED DECORATOR ELSIE DE WOLFE BELIEVED THERE SHOULD BE A MIRROR IN EVERY ROOM. A MIRROR INCREASES THE LIGHT AND THE VIEW IN ANY SPACE. WHEN YOU MIRROR THE VIEW OUT OF A LIVING-ROOM WINDOW, YOU DRAMATICALLY AUGMENT BOTH THE LIGHT AND THE VIEW. WHEN YOU MIRROR THE WINDOW REVEAL, YOU CAPTURE EVERY BIT OF AVAILABLE LIGHT AND FOOL THE EYE INTO THINKING THAT THE WINDOW IS BIGGER AND THE VIEW MORE EXPANSIVE. (SEE THE CASE STUDY PHOTOGRAPH ON PAGE 38.)

REMEMBER THAT ON A FLOOR PLAN, A MIRROR, REGARDLESS OF ITS SHAPE, WILL SIMPLY REGISTER AS A LINE WHEN YOU LOOK AT IT FROM ABOVE. IN AN ELEVATION DRAWING IT WILL LOOK LIKE A RECTANGLE.

Case Study:

In this case study, you can see that a floor plan is more than just two-dimensional shapes on a plan—it is also a great tool to help you understand your space three-dimensionally. Several factors were important to this client, so multiple iterations of the floor plan were devised. The "winning" floor plan was the one that most successfully brought the client's needs together.

Of the many requirements and concerns for the owners of this Manhattan apartment, one of the most important was that the panoramic view of Central Park and the southern views of the city's skyline be the focus of the living room. They wanted to walk into their apartment and take in the dramatic views right away. Even priceless antiques were meant to take second billing. An equally primary focus was given to their art collection. The couple also wanted the room to be flexible in terms of entertaining. They frequently open their home for charity board meetings, and they wanted a seating plan that would support a cocktail party or a dinner party, with people standing or sitting comfortably. We ultimately drew five different floor plans to address their concerns and reviewed them with the clients before making specific recommendations. You can see how each of the different plans fulfilled a different goal.

FLOOR PLAN 1. In this plan, you cannot "walk into" the view, so this solution did not resolve the clients' desire for unobstructed passage to the window with no competing elements. They objected to the alignment of the apartment's entrance with a banquette and the fact that you would have to kneel on and lean over the banquette to access the window and thereby the view and panorama.

FLOOR PLAN 2. In our second floor plan, we realized that positioning the clients' fine art above a working fireplace would have been a wonderful focus in the room. But the art was too valuable to risk the potential for smoke damage. We thought about relocating the mantel to the wall between the two windows in order to create a "dummy" fireplace over which the artwork could hang safely. But this arrangement would have detracted from the view. The client warmed to particular aspects of this plan, such as the open passages to the windows and the flexible seating arrangement. A large group could happily congregate around the fireplace, while four to six people could sit comfortably on the side, albeit separated from the center of action. However, if a small group were present, no one would enjoy sitting away from the view *and* the art *and* the fireplace. Four people might end up on the big sofa with all the chairs left empty—definitely not a positive scenario.

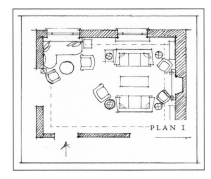

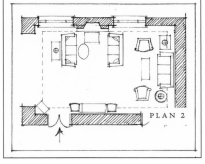

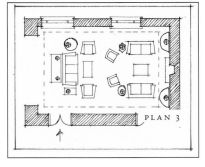

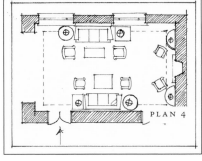

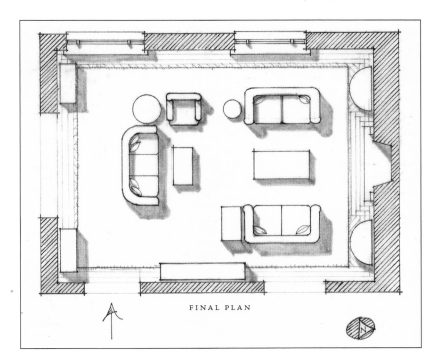

FINAL PLAN

ABOVE:
The winning floor plan boasts an unobstructed passage to the view of Fifth Avenue, a mirror over the fireplace that reflects the southern view, and a comfortable seating arrangement for four to twelve people. (Stephen Miller Siegel, architect)

OPPOSITE:
The library provides a picture postcard view of Fifth Avenue and Bergdorf Goodman.

FLOOR PLAN 3. The clients very much liked this plan's flexible and welcoming seating arrangement. Two groups could coexist, the larger one gathering comfortably, with smaller conversations for either side maintained with ease. Also, the accessibility of the window and its panorama of Central Park realized a major goal for the room. But the client objected to walking into the side of the sofa and the sofa table after initially entering the room.

FLOOR PLAN 4. Here we highlighted an interesting element of the room—its lack of architectural symmetry. As you can see from the plan, neither the entrance from the foyer nor the entrance from the dining room is aligned with the windows, nor are the walls on either side of the windows equal in length. We addressed these irregularities with a fairly unconventional floor plan. The two seating areas are centered on their respective walls but not on each other. This is a bit awkward, and it leaves the fireplace empty. Another drawback is that the room also lacks enough seating for a large cocktail party.

FLOOR PLAN 5. At this point, we continued to fine-tune the floor plan. Because this project is in New York City, we had the luxury of bringing in muslin-covered upholstery forms to try out in the room. Everyone agreed that this plan worked on paper as well as in practice. The furniture is placed three feet from the wall, providing clear passages to the windows and preserving the view of the park and access to the windows as the main focus of the room. Comfortable upholstered seating is abundant. Indeed, this room provides the ideal arrangement to support one large group of guests while allowing smaller groups to congregate. As we were experimenting with the muslin forms, it became obvious that the sofa and chair arms should stay very low to keep the views unobstructed and to add additional seating in a pinch (you can perch on the arm or the back of the furniture). Also, the sofa back is rounded and invites you to walk past it and into the room. In this plan, the couple's John Singer Sargent painting earned a prized spot on the large wall between the windows and thus occupied center stage, along with the spectacular views of New York's Central Park.

Chapter 3: The Hardscape

GOOD HOME DESIGN DOES NOT OCCUR IN A COMPARTMEN-
TALIZED WAY, WITH EACH ROOM EXISTING INDEPENDENTLY
AS ITS OWN WORLD. A BETTER OBJECTIVE IS TO GIVE THE
HOUSE AN ARCHITECTURAL AND DECORATIVE RHYTHM
WITH GRACEFUL TRANSITIONS FROM ROOM TO ROOM. TO
ACCOMPLISH THIS FLOW, OUR WORK GOES FAR BEYOND THE
BASIC DECORATING VISION OF FURNITURE, FABRICS, AND
PALETTE, AND IN FACT BEGINS WELL BEFORE THE SELECTION
OF ANY OF THESE SOFT MATERIALS.

OPPOSITE:
White-painted trim and rich
hardwood floors unify and
envelop this Colonial Revival
house on Long Island Sound.
Inspired by its location, the
owners assembled a collection of folk art and Americana with a nautical theme.
We actually managed to find
objects that were "double
whammies"—related to
both themes. A quilt with a
mariner's compass dominates
the stair wall; the marine
painting below it portrays an
American schooner, and a
pair of 19th-century mallard
decoys nestles below the
stairs. A ship's figurehead
stands proudly in the corner
of the adjacent dining room.
(Fairfax & Sammons,
architects)

The Basic Elements

The floors, walls, and ceilings in every room of your house work together in the same way that good bones form the frame underneath your muscles and skin. These interior architectural elements—what we call the "hardscape"—should relate to each other by making references to the personality and style of the house in such details as the doors, windows, moldings, trim, and hardware. We then select hard materials, such as wood, stone, plaster, and metals, and decide upon their respective finishes.

To get started, think about the location, historical period, size, and formality of your residence. Perhaps it is a very casual, shingle-style beach house. Or maybe it is a more traditional, Georgian-style urban apartment. The architectural vocabulary should not vary widely throughout a house or an apartment, but this doesn't mean that every room needs to have a consistent set of period details. Elements can and should vary from room to room, but only within the parameters of the basic style. Otherwise, you run the risk of what the design firm Colefax & Fowler calls "visual indigestion."

On most jobs, we work with the architects as they design and modify the interior architectural details. Even if you are not doing major construction with an architect or a contractor but undertaking a smaller project on your own, pay attention to the architecture and select your hard materials with care. Understanding the architectural elements and building materials used in your home defines the limits of the decorating process by helping you decide what not to use. It is not that complicated—just be consistent. This means that if you are working in a brand-new modern interior, you probably don't want hardwood floors in a herringbone pattern with elaborate borders, because they are too traditional.

"You have to see the whole. The only way to make correct choices is to have a vision of the complete architectural concept."

Floors

The first hardscape item we address in any decorating project is flooring, which can be made of wood, stone, or ceramic tile.

As you think about refinishing floors or installing new ones, take the time to analyze the traffic patterns in each room. Will people come from the outdoors into a particular room? Is it a room for one or two people (a bedroom), or is it a public room (entry or living room)? Not all public rooms have the same needs. A living room will be used less frequently than a family room, whereas a family room off the kitchen will have different traffic than a basement rec room. These traffic realities are very important considerations when you are choosing materials and finishes that have to sustain varying amounts of wear and tear.

We try to keep the floor material and finish fairly consistent throughout broad areas of a house to avoid disrupting the flow from room to room. In most public areas, such as the living and dining

Do You Know? Saddles Are Punctuation for Your Floors

When you plan your flooring, don't overlook the significance of saddles, or thresholds. Like the period at the end of a sentence, a saddle indicates a break in the floor flow. This break is usually a doorway, but it may just be an opening between two rooms. Saddles are also useful in defining the border of a floor. A wall is a natural end for a border, but at a doorway you will need to end the pattern that runs parallel to the door. Installing raised saddles at door openings is always a good idea, even if the floor material stays the same or there is no door from one room to the next. If you decide to refinish a wood floor in one room, the saddles are good starting and stopping points for the sanding and staining. Without strategically placed raised saddles, you may find yourself refinishing every wood floor in the house when you really needed to change only one room. Saddles also provide a break when floorboards change direction from one room to the next. Review saddles with your contractor or with your floor installers, who can help you by providing saddle options and alternatives.

"Architecture is extremely important. All the decorating in the world cannot hide an architectural flaw."

Opposite:
Another vista from the same entry as the previous photograph, with the view to Long Island Sound. The richly stained floors and painted wall surfaces serve as a backdrop to the owner's collections.

Left:
In this addition to an old farmhouse, wide, antique oak boards maintain the integrity of the original structure, making renovations and additions look as if they had always been part of the house. (Elliot Rosenblum, architect)

rooms, we use wood. In busy areas, such as entries or mudrooms, we most often use stone. Increasingly, we put wood floors in many of our kitchens, because even though there is a lot of movement and mess in a kitchen, the wood is easy on the feet.

Wood Floors

Wood is durable, warm, and attractive. By varying the layout, species, pattern, and finish, an appropriate solution exists for almost every space. If your home already has wood floors, consider yourself lucky, because they are relatively easy to restain and refinish to achieve the look you want. For information about finishes for wood floors, see Chapter 8. Consult your flooring contractor to determine whether or not it will be worth the trouble of repairing and refinishing an existing floor.

ANTIQUE FLOORING. There are definite pros and cons in reusing antique wood flooring, and these may either charm or deter you. Antique boards are highly decorative and convey a unique beauty by maintaining the integrity of an old house and adding instant character to a new one. They also help new additions and renovations look seamless. Possible disadvantages are that antique boards have more holes (which can be filled, of course, if you want), and the wood grain and the plank cuts may be somewhat uneven. In addition, the application of a new stain may have more dramatic results on antique pieces than with new wood. Ultimately, your choice will depend on several factors, including the style of the house, the location of the room, the amount of traffic you expect the room to bear, the cost and availability.

Reclaimed flooring usually comes in widths of 8 to 12 inches and is available in a variety of species, such as oak, pine, spruce, walnut, and chestnut. The mix of wood available for purchase, however, may include a range of different species. For example, your mix might contain 5 percent red oak boards, and you may want your contractor to remove these pieces in order to obtain a more uniform look. Like any antique building material, reclaimed floors can be expensive and difficult to obtain, so we recommend asking your contractor about the feasibility of locating the quantity you need.

NEW FLOORING. Newly milled boards are more frequently chosen for floors over antique wood because of greater availability and more uniform grain and plank shape. These, too, come in a wide variety of species. Our preference is white oak, because it is durable, has a relatively even grain, and takes a stain well. We combine two different types of boards—quartersawn and half-rift—to achieve better grain and overall color consistency. (These terms refer to the way the wood is harvested from the tree and cut from the trunk; quartersawn looks more active; riftsawn is quieter.) New boards are usually 3 to 6 inches wide.

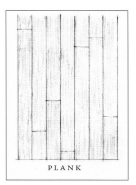 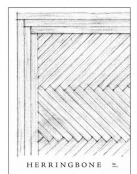 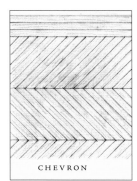

PLANK   HERRINGBONE   CHEVRON

PATTERN. Once the decision to use old or new floorboards is made, the next step is deciding how they are to be laid—whether as straight planks or in a patterned design, and with or without borders. Generally speaking, floorboards should run the length of a room and always across the width of stair treads. Patterns should not change direction on a landing; they should simply finish off across the width of the space. Patterns are particularly helpful in odd-shaped rooms; we like to run a border around the room and then inlay a patterned design within. Some typical patterns are:

Straight planks. The simplicity of this style is appealing for use in country houses, particularly when the planks are mixed in random widths.

Herringbone. This elegant motif is attractive in urban living rooms and dining rooms. We like to include a border.

Borders. They are useful in urban settings and when there is a desire to dress up a room. A border and pattern combination is also good in transition areas, such as hallways.

Stone Floors

Stone floors are admired for their beauty and character, to say nothing of their durability and resistance to water. You can specify them with confidence for entries and wet utility areas, including kitchens, baths, and mudrooms. Although the discussion here focuses on floors, we have included information that relates equally well to stone countertops, which are often selected at the same time and from the same supplier as the floor materials.

OPPOSITE:
One Cullman & Kravis signature is a preference for floorboards that are at least 6 feet long, or even longer. On boards that are of less than perfect quality, it is common to see lengths of only 2 to 4 feet, but we find that these boards distract the eye from the pattern of the flooring to the lines between boards. (Mark Finlay, architect)

If you elect to use stone flooring, remember that stone raises the level of the floor. Work out with your contractor how this may impact measurements for moldings and transitions from one room to another. In addition, confirm that all stone floors will be laid off a finished wall edge, not a mud wall or an unfinished wall, so that the pattern appears in full at the edge. If this extra measurement is not taken into account, the finished wall will rest on top of the edge of the floor and you will lose part of the pattern.

TYPES OF STONE. Every stone has different characteristics that will affect your decision about where it might best be used. When choosing a stone, remember that strength and durability are as important as color and pattern. And choose with care, because stone can be considerably more expensive than wood.

Marble. A wonderfully classic material, marble varies a great deal from one type to another and can be formal, simple, colorful, or a combination of these. Some marbles are smoother looking than others. Observe how the veining and coloration can change over the face of one piece of stone. Marble will not chip easily, but light colors will stain.

Limestone and travertine. From a purely aesthetic perspective, we love limestone and travertine for their exquisite range of creamy beige colors. But what these stones boast in beauty, they lack in durability. They are very soft, will scar easily, and should be sealed to guard against staining. These are not recommended if you want to avoid a good deal of maintenance.

Bluestone and slate. Also known as "pavers" and often used outdoors for sidewalks, terraces, and pathways, these stones are an appropriate choice for floors in transition areas, such as mudrooms, where they convey a sense of the outdoors. In addition, they are very durable and easy to clean.

Granite. Stones in this category are not generally used on floors in private homes. They are mostly for countertops, particularly in kitchens, because they are "workhorses" and can withstand almost anything.

RIGHT:
The ribbon pattern of the marble floor in this Manhattan entry transforms the space, adding energy and life. (Barnes, Coy, architects)

Visually, granite is more speckled than marble or limestone and has a limited color range.

Onyx. A type of translucent quartz, onyx is the most luxurious stone available on the market. It comes in a wide variety of colors, but it chips easily and is best reserved for powder rooms and master baths.

STONE COLORS. You can also select stone by color or pattern rather than by type. Think about a stone color in the same way you might consider a wood stain—how does it fit into your proposed environment? Don't get the flavor of the month. Choose the color very carefully, because it is not easily changeable. Some classic stones by color are:

White. Thassos, Vanilla, and Civic marble. Like a white T-shirt that goes with everything, white marbles are timeless and don't need to be changed with every paint job. White cement should be used when these stones are laid, so the color of the subfloor doesn't show through.

Beige. Crema Marfil and Botticini marble, limestone, and travertine. Of course, beige is clean and classic, like white.

The C&K Way: Stone in Small Spaces

STONE FLOORS CAN BE COSTLY, SO THE CONFINED SPACE OF A SMALL ROOM IS A GOOD PLACE TO TRY THE LOOK OF STONE WITHOUT A HUGE FINANCIAL COMMITMENT. HERE ARE SOME THOUGHTS ON STONE USAGE FOR DIMINUTIVE SPACES.

ENTRY. WITH FEW DECORATIONS OR PIECES OF FURNITURE IN THE ENTRY, FEEL FREE TO BE MORE EXPRESSIVE HERE THAN YOU MIGHT BE IN OTHER ROOMS. IF YOU WOULD LIKE TO DO SOMETHING ELABORATE THAT MAY BE COSTLY, A SPECIAL TREATMENT FOR THE ENTRY FLOOR GIVES YOU GREAT VALUE BECAUSE IT IS RELATIVELY EASY TO COMPLETE.

POWDER ROOM. HERE YOU CAN EXPERIMENT WITH SPECIAL APPLICATIONS, BECAUSE HIGHLY DECORATIVE OR FANCIFUL TREATMENTS WILL MAKE AN ENCLOSED PRIVATE SPACE FEEL LIKE A LITTLE JEWEL BOX. YOU MIGHT TRY INLAYING BRASS WITH VARIOUS SPECIES OF MARBLE OR SETTING THE TILES ROTATED 45 DEGREES WITH A 3-INCH BORDER. WE NEVER USE STONE TILES IN 12-INCH SQUARES BECAUSE THAT IS THE STANDARD PRECUT SIZE. WHEN POSSIBLE, WE LIKE TO TWEAK STANDARD SIZES TO MAKE OUR INTERIORS UNIQUE. FOR EXAMPLE, WE WILL ASK THE INSTALLER TO CUT 12-INCH SQUARE TILES DOWN TO 8-INCH SQUARES OR INTO 6-BY-12-INCH RECTANGLES.

FORMAL BATH. A STONE SLAB FLOOR IS MORE LAVISH THAN STONE TILES, BUT A SLAB FLOOR CAN BE SLIPPERY. AN ALTERNATIVE IS TO CREATE A PATTERN ON THE FLOOR WITH TWO OR THREE COLORS OF TILE AND A BORDER, OR MAKE AN ELABORATE PATTERN WITH A RARE STONE, SUCH AS ONYX.

ANY SMALL BATHROOM. USE A SMALL-SCALE PATTERN AND SMALLER TILES TO MAKE A BASKET-WEAVE PATTERN, OR USE ONE LARGE SLAB OF STONE WITH A COORDINATING BORDER.

Do You Know? Leave Measuring Up to the Professionals

YOU MAY GET THE URGE TO ORDER HARD MATERIALS FOR FLOORING ON YOUR OWN BECAUSE YOU FEEL CAPABLE OF FIGURING OUT THE SQUARE FOOTAGE. OUR ADVICE IS: DON'T DO IT. MEASURING INVOLVES A GOOD DEAL MORE THAN JUST A CALCULATION OF STRAIGHT SQUARE FOOTAGE. ONLY A PROFESSIONAL CAN ACCURATELY ESTIMATE HOW MUCH WILL BE NEEDED, INCLUDING A PERCENTAGE FOR WASTE AND BREAKAGE. WHEN ORDERING THESE MATERIALS, YOU SHOULD WORK WITH THE PERSON IN CHARGE OF INSTALLATION AND USE THAT PROFESSIONAL RECOMMENDATION TO ORDER THE AMOUNT YOU WILL NEED, OR HAVE THEM PLACE THE ORDER FOR YOU FROM THEIR SOURCE.

ABOVE:
Intricate stonework in a Manhattan powder room together with the openness of clean woodwork keeps the tiny space fresh and lively. (John B. Murray, architect)

Gray. Carrara (also considered white) and Crema Delicato marble, and bluestone. Classic gray can be elegant and cool, but it can also be cold and isolating.

Black. Absolute granite, St. Laurent and Portaro marble. Never dated, goes with everything, always looks expensive, just like your favorite black cashmere sweater.

Green. Ming green marble, slate, Vermont stone, Pietra Cardosa granite. Going with green adds some personality without overstating the date of your renovation.

Red. Rossa Verona marble. You will probably reserve red for something special—maybe a small powder room or as an accent in an entry floor. More of a statement than green, yet very liveable and rich.

STONE FINSHES. There are two primary ways to finish stone—polishing and honing. If you polish the surface, it will look shiny. Polishing also brings out the color and is more durable, but it can be slick. If you hone the surface, it will look matte and be less slippery. We often hone stones, either for aesthetic puroposes or for surfaces that regularly get wet, such as those in a bathroom. With certain limestones, we also "fill" the stone to eliminate the small holes and veins

that are below the surface and to give the stone a smoother finish. Whichever your choice, the installer can seal the stone to prevent staining, although some stones will stain anyway from red wine, grape juice, and other dark liquids or oils, regardless of the finish and sealer you choose.

FORM. You can use stone as a single slab, in a mosaic, or as pieces of tile. If stone slabs and tiles of the same stone are to be used together, perhaps in a bathroom that has stone tiles on the floor and walls and a counter made from a slab, we strongly recommend that the tiles and slabs both be cut from the same pieces of stone. Don't use precut tiles, because the color is likely to be very different from your slabs. Furthermore, if you are considering a slab countertop for a room where you are using a tile floor, confirm that the stone material is available in slabs before finalizing your materials.

Slab. This large, flat slice of stone block is cut from a quarry. A slab can be any size you wish, depending on the limits of the stone itself, as well as the capacity of the quarry. The usual thickness of a slab can vary from ¾ inch to 1 ½ inches. You can also double up slabs or specify a double-thick edge detail to make the edge appear to be 1 ¾ to 3 inches thick.

RIGHT:
Walls clad in hand-cut Connecticut field stone and exposed, rustic ceiling beams lend a tactile experience to this wine cellar, which was carved from an existing basement. Since there weren't any windows, we opened up interior ones from the tasting area into the space devoted to wine storage. A half barrel is inset into the wall at the right of the photograph. (Elliot Rosenblum, architect)

OPPOSITE:
This two-story entry hall is flooded with natural light and provides structured views to important formal and informal spaces, as well as vistas to the outdoors. The space is completely paneled and includes a coffered and boarded ceiling, with quarter-sawn oak. (Ira Grandberg, architect)

Tile. Tiles come in a variety of sizes, from small mosaics to 24-inch squares. Compared to slabs, tiles can be as thin as ¼ inch thick and may be better suited to areas where changes in floor height are a problem.

STONE-SHOPPING GUIDELINES. We always shop for specific pieces of stone by visiting the stone yard where slabs are stocked. Before you "meet your slab," refine your choice in advance by looking at small samples of available stones. When you have arrived at a few options, go to the stone yard to make your final decision, because color can vary within a given lot. Even if the sample and the slab have the same name, the stone you chose on the basis of a sample will never look exactly like the one that will be shipped to your site. Also, it is always possible that you will discover something inspiring at the stone yard when you visit in person, something you may not have noticed in the samples.

While you are at the stone yard, don't forget about the proposed stone pattern. As you think about how the stone floor relates to what you are doing on the walls, consider the scale of the pattern within the stone—the veins, grain, color variation, and speckling—and the scale of the pattern you are creating.

Ceramic Tile Floors

Tiles—and beautiful tile showrooms—are very seductive, but tile designs can quickly look dated. We stand by the credo that it is better to choose classic tiles and keep things simple. You can fulfill your need to experiment or customize through wall paint or room accessories rather than experimenting with tile work that might have to be updated in the future, at considerable expense. Ceramic tiles are ideal for children's bathrooms and informal spaces, such as beach houses. Design a pattern on the floor with your tiles or use all white tiles and let the grout lines make the pattern. An attractive floor design is a checkerboard or diamond pattern surrounded by a border at least one tile wide all around.

WALLS

Let's focus now on the basic composition of walls and how they contribute to the hardscape of your interior. When you analyze the vertical surfaces of your space, consider the length and height of the walls, as well as the moldings that will trim and accent those surfaces and the openings for doors and windows.

Plaster or Sheetrock

The basic composition of any wall in any new residential building is most likely gypsum wallboard, or Sheetrock, whereas the walls in many older houses are constructed of plaster applied to a wooden lath. A careful restoration or renovation of an older building will require the services of a skillful plasterer, although it is usually less expensive to cover damaged old plaster with Sheetrock. Plaster walls definitely have their drawbacks, because they will crack under pressure; even after replastering, cracks will reappear as a house settles. Whatever the actual

material of your wall, it is always a good idea to know (or to be sure your architect and contractor know) the exact location of the underlying studs, since they are the basic supporting elements of your room. Any heavy attachments such as new wall paneling or bookcases would have to be attached to studs, not to the Sheetrock.

Wood Paneling

The application of wood to your walls works hand in hand with moldings to accent your walls. Although consistency of architectural details from room to room continues to be the goal, variation is important when it comes to wall treatments. If one room has a specific type of wall treatment, the adjacent room may look more distinctive with a different treatment. For example, if the entrance to your house is embellished with a chair rail, the adjoining dining room might have paneling or wainscoting below the chair rail, while the living room might distinguish itself with base and crown moldings.

If you panel a room, you are in a sense creating a wooden envelope, which will be more expensive than simply painting or wallpapering the walls. But the good news is that a paneled room is very practical, because the wood will hide a lot of wear and tear.

Paneling comes in many shapes and forms and in different proportions and styles, all of which reference traditional or modern architectural styles. We sometimes worry that a completely paneled room can be restrictive, because it affects how you hang your art. Will a large painting hang over the panels, or do you want to create flat panels within the design to accommodate art? If you have large contemporary works, it may be difficult to accommodate them in a traditionally paneled room because the proportions will be too limiting. Perhaps even more important is that it limits your color scheme for years to come, because you cannot easily or economically restain a paneled room.

A great option is to partially panel the room. For example, a room could have a wood crown, base molding, and a chair rail, with paneling below the chair rail. If you build in bookcases and cabinets, you might simply paint or upholster the walls in fabric or apply grass cloth. This will let you appreciate your art on the flat surface while enjoying the richness of the wood cabinetry.

CHAIR RAILS. Running horizontally around the circumference of a room, a chair rail is a useful transition point on a wall—a visual dividing line. A chair rail can separate different paint treatments, or it may provide a break between wallpapered and painted parts of the wall. Chair rails are useful in long hallways, because they divide the narrow space both architecturally and decoratively. Applied to the walls of a powder room or other small room, a chair rail creates the illusion of a larger space.

Do You Know? A Bit of Chair Rail History

A COMMON MISCONCEPTION IS THAT A CHAIR RAIL DIVIDES A WALL IN HALF BETWEEN THE CEILING AND THE FLOOR. IN FACT, THE BASE OF A CHAIR RAIL IS 30 TO 32 INCHES ABOVE THE FINISHED FLOOR REGARDLESS OF THE CEILING HEIGHT, ALTHOUGH THE HEIGHT OF THE CHAIR RAIL CAN VARY ACCORDING TO THE PROPORTIONS OF THE ROOM AND THE HEIGHT OF THE CEILING. CHAIR RAILS HISTORICALLY FUNCTIONED IN RELATION TO THE HEIGHT OF TABLES AND THE BACKS OF CHAIRS, WHICH WERE PUSHED AGAINST THE WALLS WHEN NOT IN USE. THE CHAIRS RAILS PROTECTED THE WALLS FROM DAMAGE.

RIGHT:
A chair rail divides the walls in this two-story entry. The walls on both floors are glazed below the chair rail and papered above with Vietnamese bark paper. The floor is stenciled in a pattern that evokes inlaid wood.

OPPOSITE:
Paneling size limits the size of the art work, unless you want to hang your art over the paneling edges. In this library, the central panel was designed to accept the future purchase of a large-scale work of contemporary art. The framed abstract painting is by James Nares.

WAINSCOTING. This term refers to any paneled or boarded wood treatment below a chair rail. Appropriate in both formal and informal settings, panels lend an upscale feeling to a room, especially if made of natural-stained wood. Boarded wainscoting creates a more casual effect and is a familiar feature of farmhouses and Victorian residences. Styles include beaded, scalloped, butted, and shiplapped variations.

DOORS AND WINDOWS

The hardscape of your walls is, of course, interrupted by openings for doors and windows. There are many rules that we impose on our designs when it comes to doors and windows in order to maintain harmony. All styles of doors and windows, as well as their trim, should look the same within a room. They should also make a smooth connection between adjacent rooms and uphold the same consistency and hierarchy of detail throughout the house as the moldings do. Although the design of a door might be flat or paneled, all doors for public rooms (dining and living rooms, library, and so on) will usually be the same style. Doors for more private rooms, such as bedrooms, can differ from those in public spaces, but they should still coordinate with each other. You may change the finish on doors (from paint to glaze to stain), unless the interior of the door matches a paneled room, in which case the paneling would take precedence. Even if windows vary in shape, they too should all be the same style.

CEILINGS

Never underestimate the impact of the ceiling. The ceiling is an architectural feature that creates instant character in every room through its height and its architectural definition. And although it is often a forgotten ingredient in the design process, the ceiling is an integral part of the interior landscape.

The C&K Way: Door Illusions

MOST DOORS ARE A STANDARD 7 FEET HIGH, AN ERGONOMIC MEASUREMENT BASED ON THE PROPORTION OF THE HUMAN BODY IN ORDER TO CREATE AN OPENING IN WHICH A PERSON FEELS COMFORTABLE. YOU CAN ALWAYS RAISE THE DOORS HIGHER THAN 7 FEET TO FOOL THE EYE INTO THINKING THE CEILING IS HIGHER.

LEFT:
High wainscoting implies informality and is usually reserved for breakfast rooms, playrooms, mudrooms, and the like. In this Connecticut house, the wainscoting is painted a cream color and the walls are upholstered in a green country check.

In apartment buildings, ceiling height is generally not variable. But in a house, you can frequently find open space above the existing ceiling (called a plenum). This space can be captured to create a cathedral or tray ceiling. Even if you cannot change the height of your ceiling, you can add interest to the ceiling plane in a variety of ways. For example, you can define the space with added beams or pilasters to create structural divisions that effectively alter the feeling of a room. If you do go this route, avoid dividing a ceiling into an even number of spaces. Odd is always better; for the best proportions, use two beams to create three vaults or four beams to create five. We like to vary ceiling heights and treatments in different rooms so the eye doesn't get bored. If all of your ceilings are plain, perhaps the dining room could be coffered or the entry barrel vaulted. But do not get too carried away—ceilings should not be so varied that your house looks overwrought.

If your ceilings have shortcomings, let them inspire and guide your decorative decisions instead of hindering you. Here are some ideas:

*A very low ceiling may suggest a cramped, uncomfortable space. Instead, rather than fight the architecture, use large objects and overscale furniture. If you are in the dining room, for example, the mantel could be tall in relation to the ceiling height, the sideboard extra long, and the chandelier nice and big. Larger pieces keep a space from looking diminutive.

*Sloped or dormer ceilings may evoke a rustic barn or attic and can create a charming atmosphere. Add to the cozy feeling by keeping the walls similar in color to the ceiling. Keeping contrast to a minimum also encourages the illusion of more space.

*A room with a low, flat ceiling painted white may feel pedestrian, but if it is articulated with old rough-hewn beams, it becomes full of character and charm.

*A high flat-ceilinged room may look spacious and formal, but it can also feel cold. In contrast, a high ceiling that is dormered with rough-hewn beams can feel like a barn or a loft. Your choice of moldings, paint, soft materials, and all of your details help define the space.

RIGHT:
Don't ignore the oasis of the stair landing. Clean white paneling and trim bring simplicity to the intricate geometry of the windows and the architecture. A built-in window seat is the perfect spot for relaxing and admiring the water view. (Claus Rademacher, architect)

OPPOSITE:
The coffered ceiling in the three-story entry, visible through the doorway, contrasts with the flat ceiling of the living room. The geometry of these coffers is echoed in the wainscoting. (Mark Finlay, architect)

This Manhattan living room was carved from two adjacent rooms, which left a center beam that we disguised by coffering the ceiling. (John B. Murray, architect)

RIGHT BOTTOM:
Variations on a theme add "eye candy." In this sitting room, rich wooden ceiling beams, molding, and door trim are complemented in the adjacent room with high-paneled wainscoting in the same wood and finish. (Elliot Rosenblum, architect)

OPPOSITE:
The graceful tray ceiling in this master bedroom is detailed with white-painted beams. The flat parts are glazed green with a stenciled flower motif in the corners. (Jeff Wooley for John B. Murray, architect)

*Although it is usually the case that higher ceilings are better, there are times when we will drop a ceiling, perhaps because of air-conditioning ductwork or to change the proportions of the room. For example, in a narrow hall or a small powder room, a very high, flat ceiling makes the space feel smaller and narrower. Dropping or vaulting the ceiling plane will bring the proportions back down to a friendlier height.

Moldings

After you have made your decisions about floors, walls, and ceilings, you will need to consider the moldings, including the trim for doors, windows, and chair rails. The basic purpose of moldings is to mask cracks or hide joints. But they also provide a finishing touch and a stopping point for a change in color or finish—for example, from the wall to the ceiling or from the wall to a door. A base molding hides the edge where the walls meet the floor, and crown moldings cover the edges at the intersection of the wall and the ceiling planes. The moldings we select, combined with the ceiling height and wall length, establish the proportion of wood to wall in every room.

Architectural moldings throughout a home should be informed by and related to each other. They all have different heights and profiles, and they will vary from room to room. But there should always be a philosophical continuity throughout the house. Certain consistencies in shape will help create a common thread in the molding designs. We typically create a hierarchy of moldings, their style becoming simplified as the rooms change their levels of importance. For example, the moldings of the guest bedroom will be far simpler than those of the entry.

The height of the ceiling has some bearing on the proper molding scale, and the size of moldings will change with varying ceiling heights. For example, a room with a 9-foot ceiling will often have a base molding that is 6 inches high, whereas a 12-foot ceiling might have a higher base molding, perhaps 8 inches in height.

We usually work with an architect to relate the proportion and design of the moldings to the proportions of the rooms. An architect will also develop the molding shapes in a drawing to illustrate the family of molding forms within a single residence.

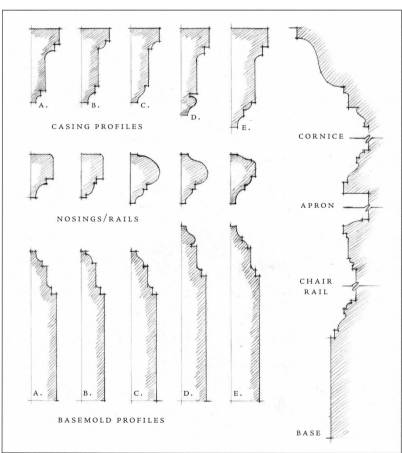

CASING PROFILES

A. B. C. D. E.

CORNICE

NOSINGS/RAILS

APRON

CHAIR RAIL

A. B. C. D. E.

BASEMOLD PROFILES

BASE

HARDWARE FOR DOORS, WINDOWS, AND CABINETS

Hinges, knobs, and pulls are finishing touches, not unlike the jewelry that finishes a stylish ensemble. And like good jewelry, good hardware is expensive. There is a lot of it in a house, so choose wisely and count carefully the pieces you need. If you already have good-quality brass hardware but the finish is worn, consider having the existing ones re-brassed. Fine hardware, including doorknobs, hinges, grilles, and backplates, should stand out as an element of sparkle.

The color and finish of the hardware should be the same within a room. On a door between a bedroom and a bathroom, where the hardware color changes, the hinge color is determined as follows: When you close the door, if the hinge is in the bathroom, the hinge should match the bathroom fixtures and faucets. If the hinge is in the bedroom or closet, the hinge matches the doorknob there. Similarly, the doorknob in the bathroom matches the hardware there, whereas the knob in the bedroom matches the rest of the bedroom.

Select your hardware early. The shipment may take a very long time to arrive, and certain pieces, like hinges, can hold up other parts of the building process, such as hanging the doors.

Doorknobs. For most of our jobs, we prefer to use round or egg-shape knobs because they are comfortable in the hand. We like simple escutch-eons (backplates) for the knobs in a non-lacquered brass or bronze. (Both metals are neutral enough to blend into their surroundings.) In kitchens and baths we typically use nickel. On bathroom doors, use thumb turns for locks on escutcheons that match the backplates on the doorknobs. Do not forget to install a keyhole on the other side.

Hinges. We like two hinges on a door with a ball finial on top of the hinges, but if a door is more than 7 feet high, we prefer three hinges. The basic kind of hinges are balls and knuckle.

Cabinetry hardware. This should match the doorknobs in the room, including the kitchen, where all the knobs, hinges, faucets, and bin pulls should match.

Scavenging Good Old Things

IF YOU ARE PLANNING DEMOLITION IN YOUR HOUSE TO MAKE WAY FOR A RENOVATION, WALK THROUGH THE EXISTING SPACE WITH YOUR CONTRACTOR TO GATHER ANYTHING THAT SHOULD BE SALVAGED. YOU NEVER KNOW WHAT YOU MIGHT BE ABLE TO USE. BE SURE TO SAVE THINGS THAT ARE OLD OR ORIGINAL TO YOUR HOME. LOOK FOR INTERESTING LIGHT FIXTURES, SWITCH PLATES, DOORKNOBS, AND OTHER HARDWARE, AND ALSO WELL-CRAFTED PIECES, LIKE ORIGINAL DOORS. DURING YOUR WALK-THROUGH, TAKE A GOOD LOOK AT WHAT IS THERE AND HOW IT IS SET UP. EVEN IF YOU END UP REPLACING THESE ELEMENTS, THEY WILL PROVIDE A USEFUL VISUAL TOOL FOR THE WORK YOU WILL DO THERE.

RIGHT:
The custom-designed "strap hinges" on this domed-top oak door are appropriate for the style of the door and the stone block walls that surround it. (Elliot Rosenblum, architect)

FAR RIGHT:
Architect Rosario Candela's 1929 doorknobs were refurbished and replated when Ellie's apartment was renovated to create a visual consistency throughout the Georgian–inspired interior.

Case Study:

Lively details in this formal house outside of Boston convey a youthful but traditional feeling. The design of the floor is enhanced with an intricate stone-slab pattern, because the entrance hall is the hub of circulation and a formal greeting space. The woodwork, including the spindles, the stair stringer, and stair risers, as well as the wainscoting, is painted white to contrast with the richly stained mahogany cap on the banister. The walls are glazed above the chair rail with a custom stencil. The painting is by Milton Avery. (Botticelli and Pohl, architects)

Chapter 4: The Lighting

UNLIKE SOME OTHER ASPECTS OF DECORATING, THE RIGHT LIGHTING IS AN AFFORDABLE LUXURY. A HOUSE CAN BE WELL PLANNED AND BEAUTIFULLY DECORATED, BUT WITHOUT PROPER FUNCTIONAL LIGHTING FOR DAY-TO-DAY LIVING AND SECONDARY LIGHTING TO CREATE A WARM, INVITING AMBIENCE, THE PROJECT WILL NOT SUCCEED. EFFECTIVE LIGHTING MAKES YOUR HOUSE LOOK ITS BEST, WHILE MAKING EVERYTHING AND EVERYONE IN IT LOOK BETTER, TOO.

THE DETAILED EVALUATION OF LIGHTING AND ELECTRICAL PLANS IS A VERY IMPORTANT PART OF OUR PROCESS. WE ESTABLISH EASY-TO-USE LIGHTING SYSTEMS WITH CAREFULLY SELECTED LIGHTING FIXTURES FOR EVERY PROJECT, AND AS A RESULT, LIGHTING IS A HALLMARK OF OUR WORK. IN THIS CHAPTER, WE SIFT THROUGH THE VARIOUS FIXTURE FORMS AS WE EXPLORE DIFFERENT LIGHTING SOLUTIONS, AS WELL AS WHEN AND HOW TO ADDRESS YOUR LIGHTING NEEDS FROM FLOOR PLAN ANALYSIS TO SWITCHES AND OUTLETS. SURPRISINGLY, THIS WORK OCCURS VERY EARLY IN THE DESIGN PROCESS, DURING THE FLOOR-PLAN AND CONSTRUCTION STAGE, BECAUSE YOUR LIGHTING PLAN SHOULD NOT BE A SUPERFICIAL ADDITION AFTER THE FACT. ONCE THE WALLS ARE CLOSED, THE ELECTRICAL OUTLETS AND LIGHTING LOCATIONS ARE FIXED, AND IT WILL BE COSTLY AND COMPLICATED TO MAKE CHANGES.

OPPOSITE:
In an entry to a Manhattan pied-à-terre, the antique lantern with swag and tassel decorations (French, c. 1800) throws general light into the foyer, while the recessed Nulux lights illuminate the Ellsworth Kelly painting on the opposite wall (pictured on the left in the next photograph).

"Although you don't need to know your specific fixtures at the very beginning of the project, you should think about and plan for the different types of lighting in the same way you think about different types of furniture."

All of the measurements in this chapter are merely our guidelines. Measurements will vary in your home, so you should make a point of visiting your site with specific fixtures before you buy them to confirm they will work where you want them. If the actual fixtures are not available, use measured elevations with scale drawings of your fixtures, or take full-scale simple paper templates to the site to confirm that what you specify will fit and will look good. This chapter is especially rich in technical information, more so than some others in this book, but we feel the right lighting it is very important, so bear with us. It will be worth your while.

Assess Your Lighting Needs

Your lighting plan is derived from your floor plan, so if your floor plan changes, your lighting plan will also change. Once the furniture is in place on the floor plan, we suggest that you "walk through" and analyze each room, identifying the types of lights you will need to make the room look and work just right. For inspiration, think about what you

Opposite:
In the pre-entry, the glazed barrel-vaulted ceiling is softly lit by a pair of reproduction bell jars and is emphasized with sparkling cove lighting.

Above left:
The hexagonal entry lantern repeats the shape of the flush-mount hexagonal lights in the vestibule of this house in Greenwich, Connecticut.

Above right:
In the same house, flush-mounted lights were chosen for this extra-wide vestibule because the ceiling is only 8 feet high.

will be doing in the rooms, and ask yourself such questions as: Which rooms are filled with or lack natural light? Which rooms will be used in the evening? Where will we sit and read? Where will we work? Which rooms will be used for entertaining and parties? Then make your choices accordingly.

Levels of Lighting

We are obsessed with layered lighting, which creates pools of flattering light for even—and interesting—illumination, and you should be, too. Layered lighting is best achieved by using more than one light source and a mixture of lighting types. These different types can be broken into four major groups: ceiling lights, wall lights or sconces, lamps, and specialty lighting. It is easy to make general lighting selec-

tions from these groups early on and, as the project evolves, to choose the style and material of the fixtures. Let's examine the different categories of lights by defining them and evaluating their pros and cons. Only after you understand your goals and options can you plan your rooms like a professional.

Overhead or Ceiling Lights

Overhead lights are necessary for general illumination in a room. They also visually raise the height of the ceiling to create a loftier feeling. Whether you use a single overhead light or multiple overhead lights in the same or differing styles, they are usually used in partnership with other lighting, such as table lamps, because on their own they can be unflattering and severe. With all overhead lights, confirm the diameter

Contemporary designers have introduced many innovative forms to the market. This chandelier is elongated in shape and works well over a long, rectangular dining-room table.

ABOVE:
This gentleman's study is a testament to layered lighting. An alabaster dish provides soft, general illumination, while a spun-brass floor lamp acts as task lighting. A picture light hangs over the Miró print and swing-arm lamps flank the sofa, as there was no room for end tables.

of the fixture in your floor plan or elevation to make sure you are considering a light of the appropriate size. If possible, test the actual light fixture in your space before purchasing it, so you do not end up with something that is too large or too small for the scale of your room.

Multiple overhead fixtures should relate to each other and be placed in a logical fashion on the ceiling plane. But as a general rule, position a single overhead light in the center of the ceiling plane (the flat part of the ceiling). If a room has a dormer window or alcoves, the light belongs in the middle of the main center plane. In a hallway, we might install one to three overhead lights depending on the length and width of the hall, and the lights should be equidistant to one another. In a bedroom, there is usually one overhead decorative light for overall illumination, while the rest of the lighting would be task ighting—bedside lamps, a lamp on a dresser, recessed accent lights over a desk, and so on. On the other hand, larger rooms, such as the kitchen, require some kind of grid of ceiling lights to achieve all-over illumination. If there is an attached breakfast area, you may have many overhead lights, such as suspended lights over the island, flush surface-mounted lights around the perimeter at the cabinet line, and a decorative chandelier over the kitchen table (see Chapter 9).

FLUSH-MOUNTED LIGHTS. These fixtures attach directly to the ceiling without a stem or a chain. They usually have a smooth, ribbed, or etched-glass cover, often with metal detailing and trim. Flush lights are fairly small, usually measuring 12 or 15 inches in diameter. Their low profile makes them a good choice for rooms with low ceilings or spaces lacking adequate overhead clearance. Use them in bathrooms, small hallways, walk-in closets, and playrooms, and as supplementary kitchen lighting. Because of their size, they do not hold much wattage, nor do they give off much light. Therefore, you will probably want to use more than one unless the space is exceptionally small, as in a walk-in closet or a powder room.

SUSPENDED LIGHTS. Hanging fixtures have stems, cords, or chains that hold the light source. There is a lot of variation in size and style in this group. Simple versions of the suspended light fixture often consist of a bowl or dish in which one or more bulbs are enclosed. The bowl, which diffuses the light, can be made in various styles and materials—such as holophane, schoolhouse, bell jar, lantern, or alabaster designs. Line up these tailored fixtures down the length of a hallway, hang them in a series over a kitchen island, or choose a single one in the center of any room.

CHANDELIERS. This type of suspended light is characterized by multiple arms, each of which supports a bulb, which may be bare or covered by a small shade. Chandeliers exist in a very wide range of designs and materials, including brass, bronze, crystal, glass, gilt wood, painted wood, and tole. Chandeliers usually hang alone and are the centerpiece of many dining rooms, breakfast nooks, libraries, and bedrooms, where they will be the main light source. Two words of advice when choosing chandeliers: First, pay attention to the weight of the piece and whether or not you may need to reinforce the ceiling where it is mounted, and second, be sure to specify a dimmer at the light switch.

RECESSED LIGHTS. We specify recessed lights with caution, because they create a dark area on the ceiling around them, and their light can be harsh and unsympathetic. There are a few instances when they are irreplaceable, such as when a ceiling plane is extremely low (under 7 feet). Recessed lights are the best for spotlighting art and sculpture and for creating a pool of light to supplement lamp lighting on a desk or next to a bed. Rather than spacing recessed lights randomly on the ceiling, lay them in a neat grid. Minimize their appearance by specifying the type that requires a very small opening. Some models even have a lens over the fixture to diffuse the glare of the naked bulb or to direct the light. Regardless of the style, order the edges of the fixture in white so they match the ceiling—or in metal, if the ceiling is not white.

"Use many sources of light in a room, each with moderate wattage,
so that the room glows at different levels and has a consistent sense of warmth."

OPPOSITE:
Sparkling crystal chandeliers
are traditional favorites for
formal dining room settings.
You don't always have to
reinvent the wheel.

Positioning Guidelines for Suspended Lights.

THE BOTTOM OF A SUSPENDED FIXTURE IS TYPICALLY BETWEEN 6 FEET 9 INCHES TO 7 FEET 3 INCHES FROM THE FLOOR (THOUGH NO LOWER THAN 6 FEET 9 INCHES). THE BOTTOM SHOULD BE AT LEAST 36 INCHES ABOVE DINING TABLES, KITCHEN COUNTERS, AND CENTER ISLANDS. ONCE THE PLACEMENT HAS BEEN DECIDED, BE SURE TO DOUBLE-CHECK THE CLEARANCE OF NEARBY DOORS AND CABINETS.

Wall Lights

Wall lights add cheer and eliminate dark shadows by forming a secondary pool of illumination on the wall around the fixture. Besides, it is more flattering to have light coming at you from different directions than from just overhead. Some act as decorative objects themselves, whether they are made of metal, glass, or wood, and they add a bit of sparkle near eye level in a room. Lights in this category include single sconces (with one bulb); double (and even triple and quadruple) sconces, with multiple arms per sconce; and swing-arm lamps.

SCONCES. Sconces are an indispensable supplement in any room. They may be new or antique, and they may be used with or without shades. When used alone, they are an appropriate alternative to overhead lighting in a room that has a low ceiling or some kind of structural interference on the ceiling. Here is the rationale behind some of the locations we choose for sconces.

Positioning Guidelines for Wall Lights

OVER THE YEARS, WE HAVE ESTABLISHED SOME BASIC RULES AND MEASUREMENTS FOR POSITIONING AND MOUNTING THE JUNCTION BOXES FOR WALL LIGHTS AND SCONCES. HERE ARE SOME STANDARDIZED HEIGHT MEASUREMENTS FOR DIFFERENT LOCATIONS:

*STANDARD WALL, 5 FEET 6 INCHES ABOVE THE FINISHED FLOOR (AFF)

*15 TO 18 INCHES ABOVE A MANTEL

*SWING-ARM LAMPS NEAR SOFAS, 42 INCHES AFF

*BESIDE THE BED, 21 INCHES ABOVE THE TOP OF THE MATTRESS OR 42 INCHES AFF IF USING A STANDARD 21-INCH-HIGH MATTRESS (45 INCHES WITH A 24-INCH MATTRESS, AND 48 INCHES WITH A 27-INCH MATTRESS)

*6 TO 8 INCHES TO THE SIDE OF THE HEADBOARD

*THERE ARE MORE VARIABLES FOR SCONCES PLACED AT THE TOP AND BOTTOM OF STAIRWAYS, BUT THEY ARE USUALLY POSITIONED AT A HIGHER POINT THAN ON A REGULAR WALL. YOU CAN TRY PLACING THE LIGHTS 5 FEET 6 INCHES ABOVE THE NEAREST TREAD, BUT BE SURE TO CHECK THE MOUNTING HEIGHT BEFORE YOU INSTALL THE LIGHTS, SINCE THE SCONCE'S APPEARANCE CAN BE AFFECTED BY A LANDING OR BY THE CURVE OR WIDTH OF THE STAIR.

OPPOSITE:
We love to call this dining room "fusion decorating." Note the eclectic mix of: an Austrian chandelier and a Japanese screen; a Chinese altar table with a Chinese bronze and Japanese baskets on top; and a Biedermeier table with Regency chairs and an Oriental rug. A rectangular recessed fixture lights the Japanese screen.

LEFT:
Empire sconces and a picture light over the Frederick Carl Frieseke (1902) painting in this Boston master bedroom create a glow above the 19th-century English pine and gesso mantelpiece. The lamp shades on the pair of oil lamps are constructed from pleated and smocked off-white silk pongee, which has been lined and interlined. Yellow piping at the top and bottom and yellow stitching knots at the smocking points add the finishing touches.

RIGHT:
Dining-room sconces placed
near the sideboard add a pool
of light and free the sideboard
surface for display and serving.
The Empire sconces perfectly
complement the Neoclassical
chandelier.

Hallways. In a narrow area, there may only be a small amount of space available for passage, and this will limit your choice of lighting fixture. Since there probably is not enough room to accommodate a table with lamps, sconces are a natural choice. Be sure that the sconces will not project from the wall too far into the hallway. Four inches is a good rule of thumb for any narrow hallway.

Dining rooms. Situate a pair of sconces over a sideboard, where they will light the food, the silver service, and whatever else is displayed. If your sideboard is large enough, you could place lamps on it, but sconces will save you the surface space for a buffet, while offering the same benefits.

Bathrooms. Flank a bathroom mirror with a pair of sconces. Side lighting is accurate and far more flattering than a single overhead light.

Living rooms. Place a pair above the fireplace mantel to accent what is always the focal wall in a room.

SWING-ARM LIGHTS. If your end tables are not large enough to support a pair of table lamps, a pair of swing-arm lights mounted to the wall behind or beside the sofa, and centered over the end of the arm, provide excellent illumination for reading. Of course, we are all familiar with swing arms as bedside lamps. We use them all the time to gain precious space on crowded night tables.

Lamps

More than mere functional necessities, lamps should add some personality and aesthetic value of their own, and we encourage you to use lamps in your rooms as you would decorative objects. Familiarize yourself with their wide range of shapes and sizes and then feel free to break (at least a little bit) from the rules of continuity that we feel strongly about in other areas. Base materials such as porcelain pottery, alabaster, glass, metal, and wood offer endless opportunities for visual variety.

Locations

Tabletop and standing lamps make up an enormous category of lighting fixtures. The chameleons of the lighting world, lamps are appropriate—and necessary—just about everywhere. Here are some of our favorite places to light a lamp:

Entries. Don't greet your guests or read your mail in a dimly lit hallway. Instead, illuminate your entry with a lamp—or better yet a pair of lamps—on a console table or shelf. If you are having a party, dim the overhead light and allow the lamps to create ambience and a feeling of welcome for your guests as they walk into your home.

Flanking a sofa. Easily accessible lighting is indispensable for reading and for conversation on the sofa, and you can't go wrong with standing lamps or tabletop versions. But if you opt for tabletop, make sure the tables that hold them are the same height. The tables need not be a matched pair, but the lamps they support should be at the same height or not more than 1 or 2 inches different in height.

Flanking a bed. Bedside tabletop lamps are essential for reading in bed and for getting up in the middle of the night without turning on all the lights in the room. The same rules apply for bedside tables as for the sofa-flanking tables: they need not match, but they should be of approximately the same height to keep the lamps at the same level.

Beside an armchair. A cozy chair for reading needs its own light source. A table with a lamp on it will work, as will a standing lamp. Look for a standing lamp designed with a bit of a table around the stem to hold a pair of reading glasses or your current book or magazine.

Positioning Guidelines for Lamps

In general, lamps should reach 56 to 60 inches AFF, a kind of middle ground between the English preference for tall lamps and the American taste for smaller ones. As this is just below eye level for most people, the lighting will not irritate your eyes or seem intrusive. Table lamps generally measure 27 to 30 inches in height on tables that are up to 29 to 30 inches high. A standing lamp is 60 to 66 inches tall, except when it is placed next to an armchair. In this case, we choose a standing lamp that is 54 inches high in the interest of comfort—the lamp will not be too high for the person in the chair to adjust when sitting down.

LEFT:
Swing-arm lights save precious space on an undersize night table.

On a desk. Do not assume that an overhead light will be enough to illuminate your workspace. An efficient desk lamp is very important for reducing shadows and easing eyestrain.

On a dressing table or other furniture. The presence of a lamp on an unexpected object helps to make the object part of the decoration of the room. For example, if a piano in a corner has just a music-reading light, it can look somewhat isolated. But with a pretty lamp on it, the piano becomes an integral part of the living room's lighting scheme. A small candlestick lamp on the open top of a secretary looks inviting.

Lamp Shades

In addition to dressing your chosen lamp base, a lamp shade softens the direct light from a bare bulb and finishes the room with a warm, ambient glow. We often create custom lamp shades. But if you lack the time, financial resources, or desire to create custom shades, you can still use the following ideas and apply them to the ready-made shades in any shop.

Materials. Every lamp shade is composed of two main materials, an exterior surface and a lining. We prefer white or off-white linen or silk shades with an off-white lining for most of our lamp bases. Although not always necessary, we like to add an extra layer of interlining, usually

RIGHT TOP:
Even though the lamp is round, we opted for the unexpected twist of using a square lamp shade in this peaceful guest bedroom.

RIGHT BOTTOM:
This lamp shade was carefully constructed to hit the lamp collar in a way that reveals rather than covers the lamp's "pistol-handled" design.

OPPOSITE:
There is no right or wrong in decorating—there is only good design. Although we make a strong case for white and off-white, black lamp-shades add a punctuation mark to this glamorous entry. (Stephen Miller Siegel, architect)

in white, as a finishing touch to make the glow more even and conceal the hot spot where the bulb is and hide the metal frame. Paper shades are another popular, and usually less expensive, option. Black and colored shades add drama to an interior, so use them only as an accent light.

Construction. The exterior paper or fabric of the shade may be transformed with knife pleats, box pleats, shirring, stretching, or smocking.

Trims. Just as we trim seams, welts, and edges in upholstery, we often accent the edges or stitches of lamp shades with trim, such as cording, drops, or knots of colored thread, particularly in formal interiors. For informal settings, we may use cords or braids made of raffia. The trim on lamp shades is an opportunity to pull out a color from the oversall room scheme and make it an accent.

Fittings. Each shade has a microsystem of hardware to make it functional. The metal frame has a cross wire at the top with a hole for the harp finial to come through. The harp is a bulb-shape wire that supports the shade. It attaches to the metal collar of the lamp just below the bulb, the finial, and the bulb clip. Harp size is very important, as it determines the overall size of the shade.

Shapes and sizing. The shape and size of a lamp shade are determined by its proportion and style in relation to the lamp base. For example, a typical lamp base 18 inches tall, with another 10 inches of height added by the collar, candle sleeve, and harp, results in a lamp 28 inches tall (which, on top of a 29-inch table, gives us the desired light at 57 inches AFF). For this lamp, we would generally use a standard flared shade with a 9-inch diameter at the top, a 16-inch diameter at the bottom, and 12 inches in slant (this would be called a 9 x 12 x 16). We have used shades that are square, rectangular, oval, hexagonal, octagonal, and even scalloped, depending on the shape of the base and the look we are going for in the room.

The proportion of shade to lamp is different for every lamp. The best thing to do is to take your lamp to the shade store, try some on, and play with different size harps until you get the height and look you want. Be sure to put the lamp on a table whose height approximates the one on which it will sit at home. When you look at the lamp, the shade should not be up too high on the candle sleeve or on the neck, nor should it allow the brass collar to show. On the other hand, it should not be down too low on the base of the lamp.

SPECIALTY LIGHTS
Works of Art

When you are working on your floor plan, consider where your art will hang in order to plan the lighting. Photograph each piece digitally and then make a small-scale copy to lay onto the elevation drawings to see how it looks. If you do not yet own works of art but intend to buy some, draw in the optimal sizes on each wall so that you know what you are looking for.

PICTURE LIGHTS. Unless a work is very large, we prefer to use picture lights to illuminate paintings. Not only is the art dramatically spotlighted, but the metal of the housing also adds a nice gleam to the wall and picks up light from chandeliers and other lights. They attach directly to the frame and plug into a recessed clock outlet. All picture lights should be 5 feet 6 inches AFF.

High-end lighting suppliers can make a custom picture light in any size and style or help you design the fixtures that you need. Picture lights are available in a wide variety of finishes. The most commonly specified metallic finishes are mirror-polished or brushed-satin brass, chrome, aluminum, nickel, and dark bronze or copper. Although many of these are baked-on polyester powder-coated paints, another coating technology uses real bronze or aluminum particles electronically polished and sus-

pended in a clear baked-on acrylic coating. These high-quality finishes reproduce the muted sheen of gold, silver, and platinum leaf that is applied by hand to many fine-quality frames on paintings.

WALL WASHERS. Recessed ceiling lights, or wall washers, have adjustable beams that can be aimed at the wall instead of on the floor like a typical recessed light. These should have small apertures; rectangular or small round models are best because the beam can be controlled. Your electrician can help you locate these in your ceiling to shed light down onto a specific place on the wall. Generally speaking, we use picture lights with traditional paintings and wall washers with very large or contemporary works of art. But this is a matter of taste.

Bookcases

In a library or any room with built-in bookcases, we often use picture lights at the top of the bookcase to cast light down the face of the woodwork and over the spines of the books, highlighting decorative objects such as china or sculpture on the shelves.

The added light will help you read the book titles, and the objects and photographs on the shelves will sparkle from the extra illumination. These lights also visually raise the height of the ceiling above the top

RIGHT:
Traditional picture lights illuminate a pair of folk portraits of the Prior Hamblen school, c. 1830. Because two gem boxes were needed for electrical power in the wall, the placement of these portraits had to be determined before construction.

OPPOSITE LEFT:
The lamp base pictured here is actually a finial from a theater curtain. Measuring 17 inches in height, it was hand-painted to coordinate with the décor of the room.

OPPOSITE RIGHT:
Constructed from a 30-million-year-old Moroccan ammonite fossil mounted on a bronze base, this lamp sits in the entry of a beach house. The lamp shade is unlined handkerchief linen in a rectangular shape, in keeping with the house's informality.

Solutions: Converting Objects into Lamps

ALTHOUGH THERE ARE MANY BEAUTIFUL LAMPS AVAILABLE COMMERCIALLY, IT IS FUN TO CONVERT AN OBJECT INTO A LAMP AND CREATE YOUR OWN TRULY ONE-OF-A-KIND FIXTURE. HERE IS HOW:

CONSTRUCT A LAMP. FIRST, CHOOSE THE OBJECT, SUCH AS A PORCELAIN VASE, A GLASS JAR, OR AN ANTIQUE TEA CANISTER. MOST OBJECTS USUALLY NEED AN ADDITIONAL BASE PIECE AT THE BOTTOM FOR STABILITY AND TO PROTECT TABLETOPS. DEPENDING ON THE VALUE OF THE ORIGINAL PIECE OR YOUR POTENTIAL PLANS TO CONVERT THE OBJECT BACK TO ITS ORIGINAL USE IN THE FUTURE, YOU MAY NEED TO DECIDE DETAILS SUCH AS WHETHER OR NOT TO DRILL THROUGH THE OBJECT TO ACCOMMODATE THE WIRING. IF YOU ARE UNCERTAIN ABOUT THE VALUE OF A PARTICULAR PIECE, CONSULT AN EXPERT BEFORE DRILLING.

CONSULT A PROFESSIONAL. ASK AN EXPERT TO ADD A COLLAR AND A STEM FOR THE HARP, AND BE SURE TO DISCUSS DETAILS AND WHETHER OR NOT YOU WISH TO DRILL.

CHOOSE A CORD. WE PREFER CLEAR CORDS WITH AN ON/OFF SWITCH POSITIONED 12 INCHES FROM THE BASE ON THE CORD. THEY ARE THE MOST UNOBTRUSIVE WHEN SEEN AGAINST A PIECE OF FURNITURE, THE WALL, OR THE FLOOR, AND THEY ALLOW EASY ACCESS TO THE SWITCH.

Do You Know? Modernizing Antique Lighting

IF YOU BUY ANTIQUE LIGHTING FIXTURES, WHETHER THEY ARE SCONCES, LAMPS, OR CHANDELIERS, THEY MAY NEED TO BE REWIRED TO CURRENT UL SPECIFICATIONS. UL, WHICH STANDS FOR UNDERWRITERS LABORATORIES, IS THE SOURCE FOR PRODUCT COMPLIANCE. THEY HAVE BEEN TESTING PRODUCTS FOR MORE THAN A CENTURY AND SET THE INDUSTRY STANDARD FOR ELECTRICAL SAFETY REQUIREMENTS. YOU WILL ALSO NEED TO MAKE SURE THAT THE BACKPLATE SIZE OF AN ANTIQUE SCONCE WILL COVER A MODERN-DAY JUNCTION BOX. IF THE SIZE OF THE BACKPLATE IS OUTDATED, YOU CAN ASK A METAL WORKER OR A CARPENTER TO MAKE A NEW BACKPLATE.

of the bookcases. Junction boxes should be mounted horizontally on the frame of the top of the bookcase, below the crown molding and just above the opening of the first shelf. In the design stages of your cabinetry, confirm that the size of the backplate of the light fits into that horizontal space. Center any outlets in the base molding of the bookcase.

Cabinets and Secretary Desks

If you have a cabinet or a secretary with glass doors in the living room or dining room, light the inside of each shelf so that the piece does not sit like a hulking dark object in a corner of the room. For a very clean and polished look, ask your upholsterer to line the inside case behind the shelves, and to cover the actual shelves, with a plain beige or off-white silk or linen. Then ask your cabinetmaker to add a small lip or fascia to the bottom of every shelf behind which a small low-voltage light can be mounted. A switch can be added to the back of the piece, or if you have a lighting system, the entire piece can be connected to a circuit in the room to be turned on with your sconces or your lamps.

When we are working with a china cabinet rather than a secretary, we often remove the shelves and replace them with glass shelves. This allows the light from the top to filter down through the piece and highlight a fine collection of china or other objects. Please note, however, that we always store the original shelves to protect the value of the piece of furniture. If it is ever resold on the market, it is critical to have all the original components .

RIGHT TOP:
Display cabinets can be lined in silk and lighted from within. Here a George III satinwood china cabinet showcases a client's collection of Chamberlain Worcester "Dragon in Compartment" china, c. 1810.

RIGHT BOTTOM:
Modern or contemporary art need not be illuminated with overhead recessed lights. Here a traditional picture light is used on an Adolph Gottlieb painting, *The Green One* (1972). Note that the frame has to be wide enough to accommodate the mounting brackets of the light.

OPPOSITE:
This pine-paneled Boston library uses picture lights to highlight Reginald Marsh's *Coney Island* (c. 1951) and Max Weber's *Nudes* (c. 1911) and to accentuate the books in the bookcase. Over the doorway, a recessed light pinpoints John Frederick Peto's late-19th-century still life.

Outlets and Electrical Plates

Use the floor plan as your guide to determine which locations are best for outlets, how many are required, and how accessible they need to be. Locate electricity sources and strategize about where additional power for planned fixtures and other electronics may be needed.

WALL OUTLETS. Outlets should be convenient and close to furniture pieces, such as sofas, beds, end tables, sideboards, and desks, but hidden from view if possible. Most are positioned horizontally on the baseboards, not above them—and never in the middle of a wall unless they are intended to service open pieces. For example, if you have an open console, you could hide an outlet behind the closed section (26 inches AFF is usually a safe height). But remember that you can never move the piece of furniture off that wall, because the outlet will show. Above-counter outlets are horizontal. If you are placing an outlet in the base on the same wall as a sconce, it should be beneath the sconce and centered to the backplate of the sconce. In bedrooms, outlets are placed about 36 inches away on each side from the center of a queen-size bed, and about 46 inches from the center of a king-size bed so that they fall behind bedside tables.

FLOOR OUTLETS. Wall outlets are the most common type of outlet, but there are other solutions based on particular needs or locations. One indispensible specialty outlet is a floor outlet. For example, if you have a sofa in the middle of a room, specify a floor outlet for lamps that will go on the side tables or for a standing lamp next to the sofa. The outlet can be placed underneath the sofa so the electrical cords may be pulled through tiny slits in the rug. Obviously, this only works with area rugs. It is very unsafe to put wiring underneath wall-to-wall carpets, so you will need to have a surface-mounted outlet cut into the carpet. Ask your electrician for recessed double sockets with screw-off tops.

Do You Know? The Junction Box

THESE ARE THE SMALL BOXES WITHIN YOUR WALL OR CEILING THAT CONTAIN THE WIRING THAT ATTACHES TO YOUR LIGHT FIXTURE. THE STANDARD TYPE IS 4 INCHES ROUND. JUNCTION BOXES MAY ALSO BE 4 BY 2 INCHES, WHICH WE PREFER AS THEY COVER MOST RECTANGULAR OR ROUND SCONCE BACKPLATES. CEILING JUNCTION BOXES ARE OCTAGONAL.

A B O V E :
Applied moldings articulate
a frame in the ceiling for the
lights, both wall washers and
accent lights, selected with
lenses in the same housing.
Works by Willem de Koon-
ing and Philip Guston are
flanked by a large sculpture
of the Indian goddess Lalita
from the Pala dynasty (11th
century) and, on the tabletop,
a Tibetan Buddhist manu-
script cover from the 15th
century. (John B. Murray,
architect)

SPECIAL OUTLETS. In addition to outlets for lighting, think about
where you need them for the television and stereo equipment, clocks,
phones, PDAs (personal digital assistants) and cell chargers, and computers and printers. Bathrooms and kitchens have their own unique
outlet issues. In the bathroom, consider the placement of a convenient
outlet for an electric toothbrush and a hair dryer. In the kitchen, consider outlets in the center island or under the cabinets or on your
backsplash for such appliances as the coffeemaker, toaster, or blender, or
for occasional-use tools, such as the hand mixer.

Cover and Switch Plates

Not all outlet cover plates are the same. For outlets positioned in
wood, choose a cover of brown or black plastic, or metal to match the
hardware in the room. Sometimes we faux-paint the covers to match

the grain of the wood in the room. For outlets positioned in stone, choose a metal to match the hardware of the room, or, again, one that is faux-painted to match the stone. On white tile, opt for a white cover. On a painted wall choose a white cover or paint the cover to match the color of the wall. If the room is wallpapered, wrap the plate in the wallpaper for a custom look. In the same way, if the room is faux-painted, you could ask the artist to paint the cover plates to match the paint finish.

The same logic applies to the colors of switch-plate covers.

PLACEMENT OF SWITCHES

It is disconcerting to enter a dark room and fumble around blindly trying to find the light switch on the wall. On the other hand, what a pleasure it is to walk into a room and have all the lights go on with a switch or two, instead of running from lamp to lamp looking for cords and chains.

There are many different types and brands of dimmers and switches on the market. Visit a lighting showroom and experiment with the devices until you find a type that you are comfortable with in a price range you can afford. If you do not have an overall lighting system, at least a few of your lights should be on a dimmer so you have some degree of control.

LOCATION AND POSITION. Figuring out the locations of your light switches is really a game of logic. For example, place switches at the beginning—and at the end—of a dark hallway and at both the top and the bottom of a stairway. Don't forget handy switches for special needs, such as a bedside switch for the overhead light and the electrical window shade. Most switches should be duplicated on both sides of the bed so no one has to get up to turn off the light.

Locate the center of switches 48 inches above the finished floor. Similarly, when connecting the control of an outlet to a wall switch, be consistent with the usage. The right side of the outlet is always the side attached to the main switch. In other words, if you plug your lamps into the right side on the outlets, they will go on and off with one switch at the entrance to the room. The left side of the outlet is always "hot," meaning it can be used for the vacuum cleaner.

GROUPED LIGHT SWITCHES. The switch groupings we recommend should always have a consistent order from room to room. We suggest that switch A should turn on the overhead light, switch B the lamps, sconces, and bookcase lights, and switch C any art or accent lights. In addition to the grouped light switches, the switches for thermostats, mechanical shades, and stereo equipment should all be grouped on the same wall, lined up horizontally or vertically, and carefully leveled.

The most advanced lighting systems on the market today are varieties of what is called the "smart house," where all interior and exterior lighting, climate functions, entertainment options, and security systems are programmed to be controlled from a single panel or can be activated remotely via a PDA device. By compressing all the switches in a room to one simple plate, these systems eliminate wall clutter. The ultimate in switching is the "hello" feature—walk in the door, push one button, and all the selected systems go on at once—and the "goodbye"—walk out the front door and turn off all the systems at once.

WORKING WITH PROFESSIONALS

As decorators, we make decisions about all the different trades every day, but in highly technical areas such as lighting, we rely on architects, builders, and electricians for their expertise. At the very least, you have to work closely with your electrical contractor, who will make sure that the wiring and switching are installed properly. Be sure the electrician has accurate information well in advance of installation. This includes photographs of all fixtures and backplates. Also helpful is a list of wattage requirements for installation (this can also serve as your lightbulb shopping list). And convey the exact locations of lighting fixtures to your electrician before he begins wiring, either by providing architectural plans or by walking through the space and marking the walls and ceilings with Post-it notes.

Once the electrical work is completed, but before your walls are closed, walk through your home to make a final confirmation of all fixture, outlet, and switch locations. It is much easier and cheaper to change an electrical location before the Sheetrock goes up than it is to patch and repaint a glazed wall.

Your Responsibility

Review all the drawings from your architect to confirm the preliminary lighting locations, and then reconfirm them against the elevations. As you look at the plans and elevations, double-check that all door swings and cabinetry doors clear the overhead lights and sconces, and remember that built-in cabinetry can affect elevations and centering of lighting (especially if one cabinet goes all the way to the ceiling). If you change something in your lighting plan, do not forget to relocate other lights so they relate properly.

Remember to keep track of all your lighting decisions in your project book. If you add a light to the plan and forget to make a note of it, you may forget to buy the fixture itself when the time comes. Remember, too, that decisions about switch groupings and plate colors are your responsibility, not your electrician's. You are the one who will be living in the space.

Case Study:

Because there is little natural light in Ellie's library, the challenge is to achieve even, general light throughout the room, as well as special lighting for the works of art and the bookcase. Certain details, such as the spot ceiling light on the globe and the fact that the bookcase light is inserted in grillework above the shelves, add a particular richness to the scheme. No less than seven sources of light are employed in this room: 1. Overhead chandelier, 2. Lamps, 3. Sconces above the mantel, 4. Bookcase lights, 5. Picture lights, 6. Recessed lighting to highlight the antique globe and 7. Window lights.

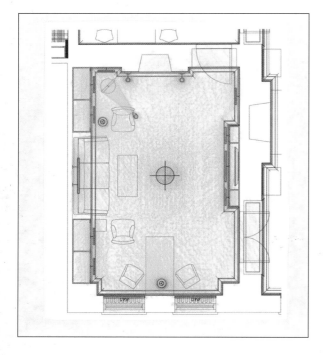

Above:
The lighting plan for the library at right was created by Francesca Bettridge of Cline, Bettridge, Bernstein Ltd. The plan visually documents the seven sources of light mentioned above. Note how the drawing is shaded to indicate the relative intensity of light.

Chapter 5: The Soft Materials

THE FOUNDATIONS FOR YOUR DECORATING—THE FLOOR PLANS, THE ELEVATIONS, AND THE DECISIONS REGARDING HARD MATERIALS AND LIGHTING—ARE COMPLETE. NOW COMES THE MOMENT YOU HAVE BEEN WAITING FOR: THE CHANCE TO ADD COLOR AND PATTERN WITH SOFT MATERIALS, SUCH AS RUGS AND FABRICS.

BUT BEFORE LAUNCHING INTO THE SELECTION PROCESS, BE AWARE OF WHAT WE CALL "THE IMPORTANCE OF ADJACENCY." IN CHAPTER 3 WE DISCUSSED THE NEED FOR CONTINUITY AND FLOW BETWEEN ADJACENT ROOMS IN SELECTING HARD MATERIALS. THE SAME PHILOSOPHY APPLIES TO THE PALETTE AND STYLE OF THE RUGS, FABRICS, AND FURNITURE. MAKE SURE THAT ADJOINING ROOMS COMPLEMENT AND BALANCE EACH OTHER WITH THEIR MATERIALS, COLORS, AND PATTERNS. TRY TO ORCHESTRATE A MIX WITHIN THE SAME GENERAL STYLE, ADJUSTING YOUR CHOICES ACCORDING TO THE HIERARCHY OF ROOMS AND THE DIFFERENCES BETWEEN PUBLIC AND PRIVATE SPACES. EVEN WHEN YOU ARE FOCUSED ON ONE PARTICULAR ROOM, ALWAYS KEEP IN MIND WHAT IS IN THE REST OF THE HOUSE, BECAUSE WHEN YOU DECORATE A HOUSE, YOU CREATE AN OVERALL, COHESIVE AMBIENCE.

OPPOSITE:
The pale envelope of materials in this room creates a welcome background for the client's important collection of artwork, including two iconic de Koonings from the 1950s and Southeast Asian sculpture. The carpet is a Persian Khorassan, which adds pattern and soft color to the room. Look closely at the pillow on the club chair—the design is inspired by a Japanese obi and relates the pillow to the apartment's theme of Asian art. On the windowsill is a 13th-century bronze of Parvati from South India and on the mantel is a stucco Ghandaran head of a goddess from the fourth century A.D.

"The living room is the center of your design universe."

Start with the Living Room

The living room is the most important room in the house. All the other rooms—the dining room, the library or study, the bedrooms—can be seen as orbiting the living room. As you move away from the living room, other rooms can decrease in their level of formality, with the exception of the master bedroom. But the decisions made in the living room regarding palette and style will impact every other room in the house.

There are two approaches you can take in the living room: You can select the rug first or you can choose the fabrics first. We usually start with the rug because the most significant purchase, perhaps in the entire project, is the living-room rug, which is usually the largest (and most expensive) object in the house. We prefer antique area rugs for formal living rooms and new woven rugs for informal or more contemporary living rooms. On the other hand, some interiors are driven more by fabrics than by rugs. If you have upholstered furniture that you do not want to replace, or if you have already fallen in love with a group of fabrics, you will most likely choose a new rug to support them, because it would be difficult to find an appropriate antique.

Rugs

The living-room rug has a huge aesthetic responsibility to bear. All subsequent design decisions flow from this rug, which sets the palette parameters for the rest of the house. It goes without saying that the rug you choose should highlight the colors you prefer, because these will be reflected elsewhere in your home. You also need to find a particular size and, if you want an antique, the right condition.

In living rooms and dining rooms, we use area rugs instead of wall-to-wall carpeting, because they add a layer of information, complexity, and detail. The area rug allows for a wooden border of floor and thus has a greater presentation value, or "curb appeal," than a simple wall-to-wall carpet. We like to have a rug in the dining room because it absorbs noise. The dining room does not have many soft upholstered surfaces, so a rug provides the welcome relief of color and pattern, which have the added advantage of being able to mask food stains.

Finding the Right Rug

The challenge is to find the particular rug that works for you. To make your search easier, consider all the following variables.

SIZE AND LOCATION. Selecting the length and width of the rug would seem to be a simple matter, but you would be surprised how the design of many rooms falls apart without the proper size rug. To find the right dimensions, consult your floor plan, which should show all the furniture in place. It is often helpful to make tracing-paper templates of different-size rugs in the scale of the floor plan. Slide the traced templates over the plan to see how they work with the furniture in position. In most rooms, we like the rug to lie at least 1 foot to 18 inches away from the wall or from at least two non-mantel walls. This is by no means a rule, but it is a good guideline.

As you work with your floor plan, consider how you want the furniture to interact with the rug. A useful guideline is to keep each seating piece, or at least two legs of it, on the carpet, which will anchor the arrangement and keep the group of furniture cohesive.

One generous rug placed under the central seating section can help organize a very large room by defining the living space and focusing attention on the most important area. If you wish to set up several different seating sections, try using more than one area rug. We do not often layer small rugs on top of a large piece of sisal or wall-to-wall carpeting, because it can look a little lumpy. But it is a popular alternative if you want a layered look.

Factor the traffic patterns in and out of the room into the size of the rug. A rug that runs halfway through a door opening may always be a nuisance; as a general rule, extend the rug two-thirds of the way through a doorway opening.

A dining room has its own specific set of issues. In choosing the size and placement of the rug, the main point is not just distance from the walls, but also the way the rug works with the table and chairs and their various con-

OPPOSITE:
It can be challenging to find the right mix of soft materials when the catalyst for the room is a rich, red Ziegler Sultanabad carpet with large, swirling arabesques. Getting the balance right in a room like this one is more difficult than in a classic modern beige space with a few throw pillows and strong pictures.

LEFT:
A simple sisal rug unifies the soaring space of this large sitting room/family room. Note the detailed ceiling woodwork and the stone mantel design. (Ira Grandberg, architect)

figurations. Set the edge of a dining-room rug at least 3 feet beyond the edge of the table, in order to accommodate the chairs as they are moved back and forth. Allow for extensions and extra tables, but leave at least a 10- to 12-inch border of floor between the rug's edge and the walls.

DESIGN. After addressing the practical matters of size and location, it is time to choose between two general types of area rugs—antique and new. The main differences are style, cost, availability, and flexibility.

First of all, consider the overall style you want for your home—formal or casual, traditional or contemporary. If your goal is a formal house, we recommend that you begin with an antique rug in your living room. This will trigger the rest of the design decisions in a formal vein, because the rug's color and style will influence the fabric and furniture decisions you make throughout your home. New rugs can also

be relatively formal if they are used in partnership with antiques and formal fabrics. Keep in mind that the living-room rug—old or new—should be the most formal of all the rugs you choose. Even in a relaxed, casual house, where we might choose a new rug of some sort for the living room, it would still serve as the most interesting of all the rugs in the house.

Affordability and availability are often equally as important as style. If cost is a factor, a new rug is sometimes (but not always) less expensive than an antique. If time is of the essence, it may just be a matter of luck—whichever you find first will be the winning rug. Sometimes a client simply does not like antiques and prefers a new rug, for which we may develop unique custom designs. Finally, if there is really only one size that works for your room, your sole choice may be a new rug designed to your exact measurements.

Antique Rugs

We have three primary reasons for admiring antique rugs and using them in the homes we design. First, each antique rug has a unique history and character and provides a rare opportunity to introduce a valuable, one-of-a-kind object into your home. Many antique carpets are works of art unto themselves, and historically may have been the centerpieces of great homes. No matter how distinctive, a new rug simply cannot evoke this same feeling.

Second, even a relatively monochromatic rug will still have subtle gradations of color. Every antique rug looks unique in different lighting situations because of the fading that takes place with age. Antique rugs look delightfully different when viewed from different sides, because of the way they are woven. Some rugs may even have faded in certain areas depending on where they have been used. The natural dyes used to make antique rugs tend to subtly transform over the face of the rug. These changes in color are a typical characteristic of the rug's natural look. ("Abrash" is the term that experts use when referring to color differences caused by natural modifications of yarns from different dye lots).

The third reason is the surprising durability of antique rugs. We do not warn our clients about how precious these rugs are, nor do we forbid anyone from walking on them. Considering that many of these rugs have already lasted more than a hundred years, we are confident that they can survive life with your children and pets.

SHOPPING FOR AN ANTIQUE RUG. The hunt for an antique rug involves a wide range of styles and prices. From national and local auction houses, antiques dealers, antiques shows, resale shops, and even tag sales, antique rugs are plentiful. Nevertheless, choosing an older rug

OPPOSITE:
The tan, coral, and cornflower palette of the Oushak carpet coordinates with the warm honey tones of this pine-paneled library. The edge of the rug extends past the chair to the door trim so that traffic stays neatly on the rug.

LEFT:
The scheme here is what we call "pattern on pattern." The printed linen on the club chairs and the curtains in contrast to the curvilinear design of the Sultanabad carpet works only when the scale of the two patterns is dramatically different.

will probably demand some degree of compromise. You may not find the perfect rug with every quality you are looking for, but the search will still be worth the effort and the money.

One unique shopping benefit that antique rugs have over others is the possibility of "trying on" the actual rug in your space. Bring the rug home to look at in the room where you plan to use it, and experiment by laying it down with the light and dark sides toward and away from the windows to see which way it looks best.

Although it is easier to coordinate fabrics with an antique rug than to match an antique rug to your fabrics, you cannot cut a nice little sample from an antique rug to take along to fabric showrooms, so you will need to get a good photograph from the rug dealer or take some close-up shots yourself. Once you have a selection of potential fabric swatches, you can either bring the rug from the showroom into your house to see how the fabrics work with the rug, or take your fabric swatches and trims to the rug dealer.

One more note: It is not essential to buy a rug based on its knots per square inch or other technical factors, but you should understand that knots and origin and condition will all affect the price and the resale value.

TYPES OF ANTIQUE RUGS. People typically think of antique carpets as the boldly designed dark rust and cobalt blue Persian carpets that have flooded the market since the end of World War II. But striking designs are available from sources all over the world. In fact, the region that gives a particular rug style its name also serves as a guide to the design of the rug. Although we don't want to be categorical in our descriptions, because each style has a wide variety of typical characteristics, below are brief summaries of the general "personality traits" that are associated with our favorite styles. These designs are not exclusive to antique rugs. Reproductions are available in all of these styles in a wide range of quality. And we sometimes use handmade replicas when an antique rug is unavailable in the preferred size or within the established budget.

Persian rugs. There are dozens of different kinds of Persian rugs, but we find that we often use Tabriz and Sultanabad rugs. **Tabriz** refers to a type of Persian rug from the area of Tabriz, one of the major cities of northwest Iran. This is one of the oldest rug-weaving centers and makes a huge variety of carpets, from medallion to figurative to pictorial. The quality of the wool ranges from simple to very fine, and the design is usually very complex and the colors intense. We especially like to use these rugs in libraries, because the density stands up to wood paneling and the massing of the books. When we use a Tabriz in a living room, it is usually the central feature of a formal room with silk damask and lots of antiques.

A very popular Persian rug is the **Sultanabad**, which is distinguished by two characteristics—coarse wool and relatively large-scale designs. Ziegler Sultanabads in particular are considered by many to be the most beautiful carpets woven during the late nineteenth century under the auspices of the Anglo-Swiss trading firm Ziegler & Company for export

to the West. In style, design, and color, they epitomize the beneficial influences of European taste on Persian carpet weaving at that time. The Ziegler aesthetic is a simplification and enlargement of traditional Persian design motifs, which in the best pieces are rendered in a soft, yet fully saturated palette. We find that the designs, which are not particularly tribal, work with a modern sensibility, and the colors are always fairly sophisticated. Also, since these rugs were made principally for export, the sizes we look for are generally available.

Another favorite Persian rug is a **Kirman**. Woven in southeastern Iran and several small neighboring towns and villages, the patterns of Kirmans are usually curvilinear, often with a medallion center and an open field. They typically have very clear colors, such as jewel tones of rich reds and red-blues and greens.

Indian rugs. If you like deep color, nothing is more appealing than Agra red. **Agras** are woven in the colors of India's jewels — rubies, sapphires, emeralds, topaz, and aquamarine. These rugs often have garden designs, floral motifs, and geometric patterns, but they may also have animal imagery, birds, and even human figures as hunters.

Turkish rugs. Our favorite Turkish rug is called an **Oushak**, known for pale colors, such as peach, coral, and celadon. Oushak carpets, with their oversize geometric, yet irregular, patterns of tracery work very well with modern art, allowing the art to be the main event. A drawback for some people (but not for everyone) is that they have a rather thick pile (furry, some say,) and the pale colors can look tea-stained, even soiled.

Other rugs. There are many European carpets, but we do not use them nearly as often as Asian carpets because they are more floral and somewhat feminine, and they dictate a much more formal room. The main types of European carpets are **Aubusson** (French in origin, flat woven) and **Needlepoint** (English in origin, also flat construction).

There is also the American "homegrown" rug—the hooked rug made from pieces of discarded clothing and textiles. We often use them as accent rugs since they are usually fairly small.

New Rugs

Even though we strongly favor antique rugs in the living room, we do use new rugs when style and other considerations are driving factors. And, of course, we use new rugs in many areas throughout the rest of the house. When we talk about types of new rugs, it is usually from the perspective of how they are made rather than their design or country of origin.

Machine-made. This group includes broadloom rugs (typically wall-to-wall carpet) and natural-fiber area rugs, such as sisal and jute. These are comparatively inexpensive and easy to find, and they can be used as area rugs or in wall-to-wall carpeting. Machine-made rugs are usually in stock or readily available and not custom colored or designed.

Handmade. This category includes handwoven or hand-tufted rugs, with either a formal or a moderately formal look about them. Handmade rugs are costly, and they may require a long wait if a custom pattern and custom colors are chosen.

Custom designs. These rugs can be handmade or machine-made with custom colors. New and unique designs can be created on the basis of an existing textile or graphic design. By playing with the scale, the color, the texture, the quality, and type of carpet, the varieties are endless.

Wall-to-wall carpets. Whether custom designed or stock, machine-made or handmade, wall-to-wall carpeting for bedrooms and other family areas is always warm and elegant. The carpeting cuts down on sound and is ideal for creating quiet spaces, especially in rooms used by children. And unlike area rugs, wall-to-wall carpets do not gather dust around the edges.

Solutions: Sisal Carpet Problems

We love using sisal because it is somehow "non-denominational." It goes with everything—it can be city chic or simple country. With an edging of cord or a binding of leather, it is run up stairways and laid down in dining rooms. And it is our perennial selection for sunroom flooring. The one disadvantage is that most stains on sisal are permanent. Even water, if not blotted up immediately, may leave a mark on your carpet.

To clean sisal properly, we call in professionals. First, they use a dry-cleaning solvent directly on the stain. Since a wet shampoo extraction method cannot be used on sisal, they will clean the entire carpet using a dry powder method. Although this does not guarantee that the stain will be eliminated, your carpet will definitely look better and the stain will undoubtedly be much lighter. Some cleaning firms may offer a second visit free of charge.

The real problem is that most, if not all, stains are basically permanent owing to the porous nature of the natural fibers. You might want to apply a protective substance to the entire carpet when it is new. This will not prevent stains, but it will allow you a few minutes to quickly blot up a spill. Remember that the sooner you attack the stain, the better your results will be.

Opposite:
The 19th-century Aubusson carpet with its vibrant reds and golds determined the palette for this Fifth Avenue living room. The gracious entertainment space is carefully edited with comfortable upholstery and striking antiques and sculpture. Curtains frame the priceless view.

Left:
The hand-tufted carpet by Elizabeth Eakins was inspired by an original document rug recolored and renamed "Ellie's Primrose." The strong colors of the rug set the palette for the room and are picked up in all the fabrics. Multiple patterns can coexist when their scales differ. We included a large-scale geometric pattern in the multicolor rug, a leafy, two-color linen chair fabric, a pair of solid beige sofas in a softly textured woven chenille, and a three-color, wide-stripe curtain fabric to keep the room lively and warm.

THE RUG IN A ROOM WITH A HEARTHSTONE MUST CLEAR THE EDGE OF THE STONE, OR JUST TOUCH IT. THIS WILL AVOID CREATING A HUGE MARGIN OF FLOOR ALONG THE FIREPLACE WALL, PARTICULARLY IF THE HEARTH STICKS OUT VERY FAR. DON'T WORRY ABOUT MAINTAINING THIS SAME LARGE MARGIN ON THE OTHER WALLS; THE 12- TO 18-INCH STANDARD GUIDELINE WILL SUFFICE FOR THE REST OF THE ROOM. BUT HAVING A HEARTHSTONE AND UNEVEN FLOOR MARGINS IN A ROOM MAY CONVINCE YOU NOT TO CHOOSE A RUG WITH A MEDALLION IN ITS DESIGN, BECAUSE THE CARPET WILL NEVER BE CENTERED. WE DO NOT BELIEVE IN SHAPING RUGS TO GO AROUND THE HEARTH.

SHOPPING FOR A NEW RUG. Finding a new rug that is right for you will require visits to showrooms. Although this is not as glamorous as attending an esteemed auction house sale or as exciting as unearthing a buried treasure at a local shop or tag sale, going to a carpet showroom is a simpler and more convenient process for most people.

Portability is not as much of an issue here, because samples will be available for you at the carpet store to take along when you are shopping for fabrics. Or, if you already have fabrics in mind, simply take those samples to the rug. If you are ordering custom colors, get yarn samples for preliminary schemes and confirm your final colors when the rug sample comes in.

In the showroom, feel confident that the salesperson assigned to you is capable of answering any questions you may have, from size and quality to design and color. He or she should be available throughout the entire process, including installation. Most show-

RIGHT:

The open grid of the Elizabeth Eakins carpet is "answered" by the tighter grid of the plaid taffeta curtains. The scheme for this country bedroom began with the hollyhock printed linen fabric by Colefax and Fowler seen on the bench at the foot of the bed. The pair of club chairs is upholstered in nubby linen with a celadon-green contrast welt and binding on the skirt edges and in the skirt pleats. Embroidered throw pillows add a small-scale coordinate. The duvet is covered in mattress ticking, which adds yet another scale in the scheme of this fabric-filled room. Note that the two most prominent patterns—the curtain check and the floral print—are separated by the solid-colored chairs and the open-grid carpet pattern.

rooms offer plenty of samples for you to choose from. Even if you are ordering a custom rug, there will be existing samples of various qualities and designs to help you make your decision. Once you narrow down your selection, ask your sales rep some questions: Is this carpet readily available? If not, how long before the rug can be shipped? Can the stock be reserved for a certain amount of time? Do you need a deposit to hold the reserve? Will the showroom order the goods or reserve them prior to on-site measurement? Will they allow an on-site trial?

Although every showroom may handle your order in a different way, here are some general guidelines to follow. For custom orders, confirm how many samples your deposit includes (some companies build in sampling costs to their prices, but others do not), and allow lead time for samples (one rug may take three samples, each one may take three weeks to make).

For every order, whether custom or not, you cannot make estimates based simply on the size drawn on the floor plan because you have to account for the way in which the carpet is made and where the seams will be. We always avoid having one giant seam running down the middle of the carpet, although it may be more costly to arrange to have two seams fall close to the edges. For a proper estimate, be sure to discuss a "seaming plan" with your supplier. Also, if the pattern is not directional, you may want to run the carpet one way or the other in the room, and this will affect the amount you need to order.

Whether your rug is custom or not, find out the shipping schedule and cost, which will vary according to the location of the manufacturer. For example, it may cost twice as much to ship a rug from overseas by air rather than by sea, but you may save weeks. Always discuss production and shipping options with your supplier or sales rep to avoid any unpleasant surprises.

LEFT:
Sometimes the only carpet solution for an irregularly shaped room is wall-to-wall carpet.

Fabrics

The palette and design direction of your home are also determined by your choice of fabrics, whether you search for them before or after you choose your rugs. Select your textiles with care, because application and appropriateness are just as important as aesthetics. Specific advice for choosing fabrics for upholstery and curtains, the two most important applications, will be discussed in their own chapters. Here we explore the topic of fabrics from a more fundamental perspective.

The world of fabrics is a huge one and can be somewhat overwhelming. There are literally thousands of choices from scores of fabric houses. Before you pay a visit to the fabric showroom, here is a brief primer on the trinity of fabric: content, color, and pattern.

Content

"Content" is defined as the fibers that compose a fabric and determine how it will wear or last in any given situation. Knowing the content of a given fabric will help you determine how appropriate a fabric is for a particular location. For example, a delicate silk taffeta is too thin and fragile for the sofa in a family room. Instead, look for something durable, like chenille. But even in a family room, more delicate textiles can be used on curtains or pillows.

MATERIALS. As with most elements of decorating, make every effort to mix the fabric content within a room, using a wide variety of textures whenever possible. Think of assembling this mix in the same way you assemble an outfit. You would not dress head-to-toe in slippery silks or heavy woolens, and neither should your room be so dressed. Here are the most common materials.

Silk. The most formal of fabrics, silks exist in an incredible array of colors, textures, and patterns. They drape beautifully and make luscious curtains. But they must be lined, because silk slowly disintegrates in sunlight. Furniture upholstered in silks should not be placed in direct sunlight either. If you are upholstering with silk, you may need knit backing for greater stability.

Cotton. Although sometimes blended with other fibers, cotton wears well and is available in a wide variety of colors and with a full range of formal and casual options.

LEFT:
Sophisticated and strong but peaceful and beachy, this Hamptons living room strikes a careful balance of color, texture, and pattern. The diamond-patterned handwoven wool carpet, created by Gregory Newham, is echoed in the diamond design of the throw pillows, which were hand-painted by Pintura Studios. Solid textures on the upholstery highlight the simple geometry of the rug.

The embroidered crewels (on the duvet, the European shams, and the front pillow) contrast with the geometry of the plaid bedskirt and the linear design of the bed linens. The simple tab-top curtains of plain linen reinforce the informal personality of this room. The blackout shades are laminated with fabric for subtle, added interest.

Wool. Good wool upholstery fabric is more costly than cotton, and it generally has the same qualities of durability and range. Tailored wool plaids and solid classic flannels are always appropriate for a library or a den.

Polyester. A percentage of polyester is added to many fabrics for strength. We prefer fabrics of natural fibers or a natural blend over all-polyester fabrics, which can be unattractively shiny. However, the industry has definitely improved the look of polyester, and we find ourselves using it quite often, particularly for window treatments.

Linen. Natural and natural-looking fabrics of linen fibers are soft and textured. Linen is not very durable. It can wear through if used on the seat of a chair, and it stains easily. Linen curtains can become wrinkled, which looks great at the beach or in the country but may not be right for a city apartment or a stylish house in the suburbs.

Leather and suede. Working with these materials can be tricky. They are cut from an irregularly shaped natural hide and are ordered in square feet, not in a perfectly symmetrical yard-by-yard bolt of fabric. So be prepared to order more yardage than you would of a regular fabric, because there will be a significant amount of waste.

WEAVE. The way in which a fabric is woven affects strength, durability, and, of course, appearance. Instead of including a technical discussion here about looms, thread counts, warp and weft threads, bias and selvage, we recommend that you consult one of the good books available on textiles (see the Bibliography). Understanding the basics of weaving will help you appreciate how a fabric will wear and what makes a fabric look the way it does. For our purposes, you probably know a considerable amount already. For example, you certainly know the difference between an airy, sheer fabric and a dense velvet. Those are two different weaves. You can definitely identify an embroidered fabric, and you can also tell when a fabric is diamond-quilted, as opposed to when a diamond design has been printed or hand-painted on a smooth fabric. Damask is a more complicated weave, usually woven as a frame around a floral centerpiece design, often with side elements. A plaid is a geometric weave created by mixing different colored threads in different proportions. We prefer woven damasks and plaids to the printed variety. Generally speaking, printed plaids and damasks are less dressy than woven ones.

Color

Although you may be guided by a carefully considered palette for your house, color is one area where the temptation to make an emotional decision rather than an intellectual one is quite strong—and that can be a very good thing. When we look at a single fabric, we classify it according to whether it is predominantly one color or multiple colors. It is helpful to have an understanding of color theory before you make decorating decisions. If you are unfamiliar with the concept of the color wheel, you may wish to consult a color theory book for guidance (see Bibliography). We will explore in more detail how color applies to upholstery and curtains in later chapters.

Pattern

Pattern is the visual design of a fabric. Patterns can be woven directly into the fabric, printed onto one side of the fabric, or applied to the fabric in some other way (see "Embroidery" and "Paint" below).

Solids. Actually a patternless pattern, solids are the chameleons of the fabric world. When working with a solid fabric, pay attention to the weave—different weaves and content are what differentiate the solids from each other. For example, two beige fabrics, one a silk velvet and the other a linen herringbone, are the same color, but they convey very different messages. The velvet would look elegant on a formal living-room sofa, whereas the woven linen could work as a less formal table skirt or on a side chair in a bedroom.

Plaids and stripes. Plaids and stripes can be woven or printed, tonal or multicolored. They are cheerful, traditional additions to almost any room. In embellished stripes and plaids, some sort of figure, such as a sprig or leaf, is interjected into the base pattern. Use these casual patterns in kitchens and for occasional pillows. A small-scale, variegated stripe is known as a *strié*.

Damask. Damask is characterized by lush floral or scrolling designs in one or two colors. Damasks in silk and wool are dressier and thus ideal for living rooms, whereas cotton and linen damasks are more casual and appropriate for bedrooms. True damask is always woven, although damasklike patterns are sometimes printed onto fabric.

Curvilinear designs. Whether simple or complex, designs of floral patterns, scrolls, paisley, or vines can be printed (as on toile and chintz) or woven. (The word "chintz" refers to a shiny finish on a cotton fabric.) We like to mix curvilinear patterns with the geometry of stripes and plaids.

Embroidery. Crewel and line embroidery patterns are sewn directly onto the fabric. When sewn by hand, embroidered fabrics can be expensive, but we try to use them often—on everything from chairs to pillows and curtains—because of their value as one-of-a-kind works of art. One especially decorative approach is to use metallic threads for the embroidery, as well as in trimmings. With intricate designs, we like to supply the artist with neutral ground fabrics, such as linen, silk, or a smooth wool. Machine-embroidered fabrics can also be expensive, but they are worth the investment. Use them on a pillow or a side chair or as a duvet cover for your master bed.

Paint. We sometimes have artists paint patterns on fabrics for a special, unique effect. Any pattern noted above can be painted or stenciled. The advantage is a completely custom fabric that is not available in the marketplace

Establishing a Fabric Scheme

Once you understand the fundamentals of fabric, the real challenge is to filter through the jumble and build a harmonious mix of fabrics. To do this, create a fabric plan for the interior, which we call a scheme, based on an assortment of color and palette, content and texture, and pattern and scale. In assembling a room scheme, the goal is for a refined combination of all these things, which is a very subtle achievement. Again, it is somewhat like getting dressed, as, for example, when a man pairs a colored and patterned silk tie with the scale and color of the check of his dress shirt and with the scale of the pinstripe in his suit.

Begin by choosing a general direction—i.e., monochromatic, two-colored, or multicolor. Then select fabrics based on the palette and style preferences. If the overall look is traditional, you might look at patterns. If the overall look is modern, try exploring textures instead. Analyze how all these variables will affect the mood and look of the interiors as you narrow down your fabric options until you reach a comfortable balance. Although there are no hard and fast rules to shopping for fabrics, we stand by the following principles:

*Always have a solid in the room to give your eye a place to rest.

*Include a mix of pattern and texture in every room.

*Vary the scale of the patterns within a room by using what we call "small-scale coordinates." These are fabrics with small geometric, trellis, diamond, or flower patterns of various colors that can be used anywhere in a room. They serve as bridge fabrics between the solids and large-scale patterns of the curtains and the large upholstered pieces, and are useful on side chairs, pillows, seat cushions, or ottomans.

*Do not use your main fabric on more than three items in a room.

*Do not use the same mix of fabrics for adjacent rooms.

Upholstery and Curtain Trim

We use trim—a subset of fabric—to finish seams. There are many readily available trims, but for aesthetic reasons, we often custom-color them if we cannot find the right color for the scheme. When you trim your curtains and upholstery, you are accessorizing and customizing your interiors.

Cord. This is the most basic type of trim. You can always use a fabric welt, but we prefer cord around the edges and in the seams of all sofas and club chairs. A typical sofa can have 30 yards of cord. When used like this, it has a tape edge, machine-sewn into the seams. Conversely, on a curtain, the cord would be used without a tape edge and be sewn onto the front and bottom edges of the curtain panels. The basic kinds of cord are plain, plaited, and crepe.

Gimp. This is a braid used as trim to cover the upholstery tacks on furniture with a wooden frame.

Nail heads. These come in a wide variety of finishes and sizes, and can also be used to hide the tacks and make a decorative edge. Sometimes we use nail heads on top of the gimp, but their diameter must be smaller than or equal to the width of the braid.

Tape. This is another flat type of upholstery trim, used for curtain and skirt edges. Tape looks best when it is set in from the edge of the skirt or curtain edge rather than set right on the edge. Set it in by about ¾ inch, or the width of the tape itself. A decorative tape can also be applied on the face of a pillow.

Fringe. Whether looped or cut or tasseled, fringe is used in seams or on top of them. We use fringe more on curtains and pillows than on seating. A tassel fringe can be made from fabric threads or some sort of beads—wooden or crystal—which hang down off a tape edge. Tassels look best on curtains and pillows. For a really luxurious effect, run the tassel twice around the outside edge of a pillow. Bullion is a long, heavy fringe used at the bottom of a skirt. Typically, the length of the bullion equals the length of the skirt. If the bullion hangs in front of a fabric skirt, use one layer of bullion. We like to use two layers of bullion and eliminate the skirt.

Curtain trim is traditionally applied along the bottom edges of valances and along the bottom and leading edges of curtain panels. When there is a center curtain panel, trim goes around the panel's three edges. On a Roman shade or other type of shade, we would run the trim, usually a tape, around the two sides and the bottom edge. An important consideration with curtain trim is the weight of the trim and how it affects the way the curtains hang. Some trim will be too heavy and will ruin the drape of the fabric, whereas other styles need the weight to maintain their shape.

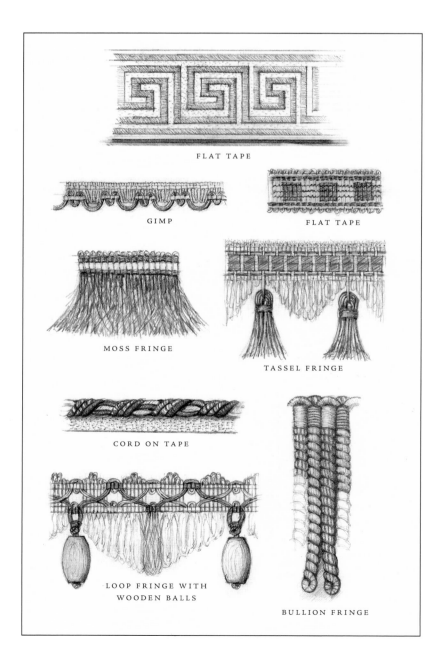

FLAT TAPE

GIMP

FLAT TAPE

MOSS FRINGE

TASSEL FRINGE

CORD ON TAPE

LOOP FRINGE WITH
WOODEN BALLS

BULLION FRINGE

Shopping for Fabrics

Aesthetics aside, there are some significant practical points to know before you go shopping for fabrics. Solid or striped, cotton or wool, all fabrics have some common technical points. Learn these terms, regardless of which fabrics you choose or where you plan to buy them, because they directly affect your upholstery or curtains.

Width. Bolts of fabric come in set widths. Most fabrics are around 54 inches wide.

Repeat. This term refers to the measurement that reflects the pattern and how often it repeats itself horizontally or vertically over the fabric. Solid fabrics have no repeat; a small stripe might have just a 2-inch repeat; a damask may have a 23-inch repeat horizontally and then a vertical repeat or "drop." The information regarding a fabric's repeat is found on the fabric label and should be given to your upholsterer or curtain maker, because there are measuring implications. Additionally, because of their repeat measurement, certain fabrics should not be used for certain projects. For example, if your choice has a 32-inch repeat, that means it appears only once across the standard 54-inch width of the fabric. If you center the pattern on the face of a sofa-back pillow, you will have a fair amount of waste and lose a critical amount of the design. This may or may not matter to you.

Scale. Always consider the scale or size of the pattern relative to the others in the room. Think of a tiny check as a small-scale fabric and a bold damask as a large-scale fabric.

Yardage. This is the amount of fabric required for a particular project based on all the above measurements, with accommodation made for some degree of waste. Never estimate yardage yourself. Let your upholsterer or curtain maker provide you with this figure based on the shapes of your upholstery and the design of your curtains.

Making a Selection

Now that you have your fabric scheme and an understanding of the technical issues involved in fabric manufacture, it is finally time to get out and actually buy some fabrics! Shopping for fabric is one of the most active and enjoyable parts of every project. Although there are no hard and fast rules for shopping, you will want to be efficient and feel smart as you venture into the fabric showrooms. What follows is a quick shopping guide.

If you live in a metropolitan area, you may have access to large fabric showrooms that sell "to the trade" only. (This means that you can come in and look but will not be able to take samples home, unless you have a decorator who can call ahead on your behalf.) If you live outside the city, your only option may be a local shop that carries fabric books from many different suppliers.

Try to educate yourself about fabrics before you walk into a shop to look at the various options. You can start by looking at the fine print in the shelter magazine articles, which always include information about where fabrics are from. Showrooms often supply pads and pencils for you to record the samples that you like. Although there is no charge to check out samples, there is usually a limit on how many you may take out and a date by which you will have to return them.

Remember that multicolor fabric samples don't necessarily show the whole pattern and color of the fabric. A red-and-brown plaid that appears to be predominantly brown in a small sample may have more red in it when you see the entire pattern laid out on a 7-foot sofa. With multicolor fabrics, request a large memo sample before you order to avoid any misconceptions about the color.

Most fabrics, even solids, can change color depending on the light in which you look at them. It's worth ordering a yard or so of fabric to examine in different lighting situations. We don't do this with everything, but if you are about to order thirty yards of fabric for curtains or twenty yards for a pair of sofas, it's a good idea to confirm your choice before you send in a deposit.

When we shop, we bring little swatches of whatever we have chosen so far, such as pieces of yarn from the rug, paint chips, a small cutting of fabric from something already existing, and perhaps even a photograph.

You can staple all of these objects to a piece of vellum and slip it inside a plastic sleeve. We call these our cut sheets, and we add to them as we make selections. If you are shopping for more than one room, keep all the plastic sleeves in a binder to help you be more organized (see page 216).

A few more practical hints: Wear comfortable shoes, bring water, stop for lunch or a snack, and do not wear a heavy coat. Fabric shopping can be very tiring, and you should make the most of a long day by being prepared for it.

Purchasing Your Fabrics

There will be many opportunities to check and double-check your choices along the way, but there are a few final checkpoints when you reach the point of actually placing your fabric order. Once you are ready to commit, here is how to complete your purchase with peace of mind.

CFA. Ask for a "cutting for approval" (CFA), before you approve your order. This is a cutting from the exact bolt from which your stock will be cut. Examine all CFAs to make sure that they are correct (fabrics are occasionally mislabeled in showrooms, and human error sometimes

OPPOSITE:
Tyes of upholstery and curtain trim

LEFT:
The large scale of the blue-and-white plaid in the handwoven carpet is offset by the smaller-scale check of the yellow-beige curtain fabric. Shades of blue, beige, and off-white come together in the hand-painted stripe on the wall, the curvilinear floral fabric on the chair and the ottoman, and the plaid fabric on the bed.

ABOVE:
Often keeping a scheme
simple in one respect—in this
case the color red—allows a
variety of patterns to coexist.
Toile envelops this room
while vibrant red checks
accent the twin beds.

OPPOSITE:
Decorative cord, both
blocked and solid, finishes
the upholstery seams on the
club chair in the foreground,
the seat cushion on the caned
chair, and the sofa cushions.
Jim Dine's *Robe with Red Sash*
(c. 2000) surveys a Pembroke
table and a caned mahogany
chair, both George III.

Do You Know? The Authenticity of Documentary Fabrics

IF, IN YOUR EFFORT TO MAKE A NEW HOUSE LOOK OLD, YOU HAVE GONE TO
THE TROUBLE OF USING HISTORIC STYLES OF ARCHITECTURE, HARDWARE,
AND WOODWORK, YOU MIGHT ALSO WANT TO USE TEXTILES THAT REFLECT
THE STYLE OF THE HOUSE. THIS IS QUITE EASY TO DO BECAUSE MANY OF THE
FABRIC SHOWROOMS HAVE DOCUMENTARY FABRICS WHOSE DESIGNS ARE
BASED ON SIGNIFICANT TEXTILES FROM THE ARCHIVES OF MUSEUMS AND
HISTORIC HOUSES. SOME SHOWROOMS EVEN HAVE THEIR OWN ARCHIVES.
THEIR DESIGNERS ALTER THE SCALE, THE REPEAT, AND OFTEN THE COLORS
TO CREATE NEW FABRICS THAT ARE INTERPRETATIONS OF HISTORIC DESIGNS.
THE SALESPEOPLE CAN GUIDE YOU TO THE RIGHT FABRICS FOR YOUR PROJECT
BASED ON THE PERIOD OF YOUR HOME, THE STYLE OF YOUR FURNITURE, AND
THE WAY YOU LIVE. ALTHOUGH YOU PROBABLY WOULD NOT USE THEM ON
EVERYTHING, DO NOT BE AFRAID TO DISTINGUISH A PIECE OF UPHOLSTERY
WITH THE SIGNATURE OF A DOCUMENTARY FABRIC

ABOVE:
This country living room has a broad mix of fabrics—curtains fashioned from hand-printed silk in a batik-inspired design with lush chenille and patterned velvet on the sofa and slipper chairs. The punch is provided by terra-cotta-colored silk on the Napoleon III side chair, especially by the printed leopard silk velvet on the tufted ottoman.

RIGHT:
This picture shows the importance of edging details. The pillow has a contrast cord with the flange sewn into the seam, so you see only the decorative cord. On the face of the pillowcase, two rows of decorative tape hide the seam between the two fabrics. The openness of the hand-painted curtain fabric lightens the effect of the woven damask on the chair and the elaborate pillow treatment.

OPPOSITE:
The large-scale plaid taffeta used for the curtains in this country house adds a note of informality. The carpet is an antique Turkish Ottoman Empire rug in the Arts and Crafts style, c. 1900.

occurs on order forms) and also to make sure that the dye lot (the current batch of fabric being produced at the mill) matches the sample you fell in love with. Sometimes ground colors can vary, particularly with natural linen, which can turn up a little too pink or too green for your color scheme.

FABRIC PROTECTION. If you are concerned about fabric durability, you may want to have your fabrics specially treated to make them resistant to staining. There are many methods of doing this (including Scotchgard and Fiber-Seal), and the treatment should not change the quality of the fabric in any way. If you are nervous about this, however, send a small piece as a sample to the treatment facility. It is not necessary to treat every fabric, but fabrics intended for high-traffic areas, such as dining-room chairs, a kitchen sofa, and playroom furniture, are all good candidates.

LEAD TIME. When you order, the mill will give you a lead time for the fabric's availability. It may be in stock, or it may have a lead time of several weeks. Coordinate the arrival of the fabric and the completion of the upholstery and curtains for the dates you want to install. If your upholstery has a six-week lead time upon receipt of the fabric, and the fabric is ten weeks out of stock, you will not have furniture for at least sixteen weeks. This is very common. Do not be alarmed—just be aware that it can happen.

CASE STUDY #1 (OPPOSITE):

The inspiration for this bedroom was the Bennison "Shangri-la" printed linen fabric, which the owner fell in love with. Because this room was driven by fabric rather than by the carpet , we turned to Gregory Newham, who created the geometric, hand-dyed and handwoven carpet pictured here in shades of cream, rose, and blue. The walls were covered in cream-color linen damask and the curtains have an unexpectedly bold red-checked lining. The solid taupe velvet upholstery on the chaise near the window adds a note of calmness.

CASE STUDY #2 (BELOW):

This living room is an example of a carpet-driven rather than a fabric-driven scheme. The genesis for the palette of this room, as well as for the entire house, came from the very rare and early nineteenth-century Persian Lavar Kirman carpet, which has an unusual garden design in reds and yellows. The juxtaposition of a floral European-influenced border with a more traditional Persian tree design is quite original. Also note the sinuous renderings of the trees, which add graceful movement.

Chapter 6: The Upholstery

SIFTING THROUGH STYLES OF UPHOLSTERED FURNITURE SHAPES
AND ENVISIONING THEM IN THE FABRICS YOU HAVE CHOSEN IS
ALWAYS ONE OF THE MOST CREATIVE CHALLENGES. THIS MARRIAGE
OF FORM WITH COLOR AND TEXTURE IS MORE THAN JUST A
QUESTION OF AESTHETICS—IT IS ALSO A MATTER OF COMFORT.
AND ONCE YOU UNDERSTAND THE VARIABLES, YOU WILL BE ABLE
TO MAKE AN EDUCATED DECISION WITH CONFIDENCE.

OPPOSITE:
A monochromatic palette
does not have to be cream or
white but can be saturated
with color, as it is in this
room. The Odom chair was
named for its designer, William Odom. When covered
in strié velvet with contrast
cord in the seams, it is
elegant and formal. A Robert
Motherwell painting, *Chinese
Emperor*, surveys the scene.

Selecting Furniture Forms

Practical Considerations

The following concepts will help you narrow down your options:

COMFORT. Because we want the interior of a house to look good, the real challenge we face is to find well-designed furniture that is comfortable. Always sit down in a piece, whether it is brand new or an antique, before you commit to buying it (see more about this in "Working with an Upholsterer," page 121). How the furniture will be used also has some bearing on its comfort level. For example, we all have different expectations about a cushiony chair for curling up in and reading or watching television in a family room than we do for a more formal chair required for sitting up straight in a living room.

Like us, you should be fully committed to comfort. If you are drawn to the way a particular chair or sofa looks, but it feels like a rock when you sit down, try to solve the problem by changing the type of fill used inside. Foam is very firm and springy, while down is very soft. But a combination of 80 percent down and 20 percent foam is a happy medium.

DESIGN. Consider the overall silhouette of a piece and its geometry with relation to four main elements—the arms, the back, the cushions, and the legs. The arms may be scrolled or square in shape; they may be upholstered or not. The back may also be scrolled, or perhaps rounded or squared. The cushions may be tight or loose. The legs may be on view or hidden behind a skirt of fabric or bullion fringe. They may be made of wood or upholstered.

LOCATION AND SCALE. Notice where each piece of furniture sits in relation to the others. Pieces next to each other should not have all the same details, but neither should their components be so different that the pieces fail to communicate with each other.

RIGHT:
In the same living room as that illustrated on the previous page, a large and comfortable Bridgewater sofa with a set-back arm is also covered in the same strié velvet. The bullion fringe at the base of the sofa is embellished with tassels. Bullion is practical, because heels won't mark the fabric as they would on a regular skirt. The throw pillows are covered with antique textiles.

OPPOSITE:
The pair of scroll-back Odom chairs on the right, whose skirts have double-inverted corner pleats, is upholstered in a small check. Although the rug and the chairs both have checked patterns, the scale of each is different, so that they work together. The closed mass of the sofa, which has a skirt with a tape detail at the bottom, is offset by two unmatched antique wooden chairs and a pair of tiny wooden footstools in front of the Odom chairs.

Is the sofa flanked by two chairs? If so, the chairs can be a pair while the sofa stands alone. If the sofa has a skirt, the pair of chairs might look better with exposed wooden legs. Equally important is how your upholstery relates to the architecture of the room. Is the chair next to a window or another chair? Do you walk into the room into the back of a long sofa or into the back of a pair of chairs? If so, perhaps they should not have high backs. As you choose your furniture forms, double-check the flow of the room and the flow of your house as you initially established it on your floor plan.

Embrace the idea of scale and make it work for you. Just because a room is enormous does not mean that the furniture pieces should be oversize. Seating pieces should always be on a human scale, generous and comfortable for everyday use. Compare the size of each piece to the other upholstery, to the tables and chests, and to the overall room. Mix and balance the pieces within each room as you try to keep a consistent volume of furniture within every room. One room, for example, should not be relatively empty or filled with dainty pieces next to a room with an oversize sofa and two big club chairs. This can produce a jarring contrast. With time and experience, you will not be afraid to add that one final piece in the "wrong" scale—either too large or too small—that gives your room a special character.

Upholstered Furniture Types

In choosing upholstered furniture, we look at three main categories—custom, ready-made, and antique. Your own choices depend on the style of furniture you like (new or old, modern or traditional), as well as on the importance of the room (a formal living room or a casual family room) and the ease or difficulty of finding just the right piece.

CUSTOM FURNITURE. Without question, we prefer to order custom upholstered furniture from an upholsterer rather than to purchase ready-made pieces, and we usually specify custom work in all the rooms

we design. By custom, we mean upholstered seating pieces, including ottomans and dining chairs, that can be adapted and ordered to suit your needs in terms of overall size and shape, types of arms and legs, the slant of the back, the depth and fill of the seat and back cushions, details such as trim or nail heads, and so on. You will probably pay a premium to work with an upholsterer, but you should be able to trust the firm's expertise and expect them to help you with your decisions. Ordering custom furniture may be more time consuming and costly than finding furniture in a store. But like the fit of a couture dress or the seams on a tailor-made suit, custom upholstery promises comfort while it allows us the freedom to control the most minute elements of the designs.

There are many forms of sofas and chairs, but we have come to trust the comfort and style of a few classic forms. We feature them often in principal rooms, altering the upholstery details as we see fit. Here are a few of our favorite types:

Bridgewater chair and sofa. If you are looking for a relaxing chair or an ample sofa with a club-room look, the Bridgewater style is an excellent choice, because it looks as if it belongs in a library at Harvard or a British club. This form is traditional in leather, but it is particularly well suited to wide-wale corduroy with nail-head trim and its wood legs on show.

Jean-Michel Frank–style chair and sofa. Based on a form created in the 1930s by French designer Jean-Michel Frank, this chair and accompanying sofa have very clean modern lines that translate well to a variety of different interior styles. For instance, we have successfully paired this sofa with Arts and Crafts pieces from the 1890s, as well as Art Deco and other French furniture from the 1920s into the 1940s. We usually specify that the arms be slightly reduced from the original 6-inch width to a 4-inch width in order to lighten up the overall scale.

Odom chair and sofa. This form has a rounded front and works well in a tight spot or a narrow room. With its high back, the sofa is best against a wall, but the rounded front of the chair is good floating in the center of the room.

Paley chair and sofa. This graceful sofa floats well in the center of the room, where the swooping scrolled arm is just the right size, and it looks good from every angle.

Carr sofa. This sofa is the most versatile and works in nearly every environment, from a living room to a library. When you think "sofa," an image of the Carr is what will most likely pop into your head.

C&K sofa. This sofa is our own design, an evolution of the Carr in which we have amended the measurements to work better with antique seating pieces, such as wing chairs. Our form has a higher back, so the proportions work better.

"Personality" chairs. Not every piece in a room should be of the same scale. In fact, we firmly believe in varying the scale of upholstered furniture in every room. A "personality" chair often fits the bill when we do not want to use an antique chair or a settee. A slipper chair, for example, works well in a bedroom. But if you increase the scale and add a scroll back, it also makes a useful chair in a living room next to a sofa and opposite an antique wood-framed chair.

Ottomans. When used with a club chair, an ottoman will share the same upholstery details. We do not use shaped ottomans, because they tend to make the chair look like a big chaise that belongs in a bedroom. The rectangular form of the ottoman is more flexible and can go anywhere in a room. Add casters to the legs for mobility. When designed to stand alone, as a kind of soft coffee table, our favorite ottoman is tufted or the fabric is mitered on top with visible nail-head trim and wooden legs. Do not use casters on these ottomans, because it is best if they do not move around too easily.

OPPOSITE:
The two pairs of Paley chairs flanking the fireplace have visible wooden legs with casters only on the front legs so that the chairs don't move around. The open legs and the space around the upholstered chairs prevent this cozy sitting room from being eaten up by the mass of upholstery.

LEFT:
In the billiard room of a beach house, we upholstered a Jean-Michel Frank sofa in beige-textured linen rather than the more expected leather. Bridgewater chairs with exposed legs and casters benefit from the clean caramel leather upholstery, while the shaped scroll-back chair on the right has a tufted back with a subtle damask fabric. Note that the matching lamps sit on an unmatched pair of tables in the center of the room. Although not identical, the tables are of the same height to insure that the lamps are also at the same height, thus avoiding a sense of unbalance in the room.

READY-MADE SEATING. You can tailor your seating to a certain degree by working with a retail store. Many stores will let you make slight changes to their standard pieces, often for an extra charge. But consider the added cost a worthwhile investment, because upholstered pieces are such an important component in your rooms.

When it is not possible or desirable to create custom pieces for a client, we appreciate the convenience of ready-made furniture. For a luxurious look without the expense of custom work, purchase a ready-made retail piece with a great silhouette and reupholster it in a different fabric.

It is very difficult to determine what you are really paying for when you buy ready-made furniture, because most of the furniture piece is hidden from view. However, you can look for the following: Determine whether or not the frame is made of hard wood rather than plywood, pressed wood, or cardboard. Make sure that you have hand-sewn coil springs rather than zigzag springs, a one-piece mechanism. And make certain that all the cover fabric matches properly. The rest is up to the honesty of the manufacturer.

ANTIQUE SEATING. Given our devotion to antiques, you might expect Cullman & Kravis to specify antique furniture as our first choice in furnishings. The truth is that we would never design a room using only antique seating pieces, primarily because period furniture is not always comfortable. The seats can be re-sprung, but the pitch and the other ergonomic measurements may not be as comfortable for modern-day users as we would like. Antique seating can also be expensive, which makes it better suited for accent pieces that add variety and interest. Once we have a certain number of comfortable seating areas in a room, we will add antique chairs, a bench, or maybe a settee to create an interesting mix.

FAMILY "HEIRLOOMS." Not every project starts from scratch. Most people have some pieces they want to keep and reuse. These may include hand-me-downs that deserve a new lease on life rather than being given away to the thrift shop. Before you get rid of your aunt's old sofa, ask your upholsterer if he can re-invent it. If the frame is good—both sturdy and intact—he can probably restuff the cushions, restain the legs, and

RIGHT:
The typical arm of this C&K sofa is scrolled with a center panel, which we often trim in cord. The arm comes neatly to the front of the platform to avoid a T-shaped seat cushion.

OPPOSITE:
The sofa pictured is ready-made. Upholstered in the customer's own material, it does not look as if it came "off the rack." (Jacquelyn Robertson, architect)

reupholster the piece in new fabric, so that you will end up with a "new" sofa. If you like the basic style but are not sure about the legs, try adding a skirt or a bullion fringe to hide the legs. With all of the options available, there is usually a way to transform something old into a new piece that you will love.

Upholstery Options

You are not done yet. There are still a multitude of details to iron out. Most of these options require identification and selection, if you are ordering a custom piece. But even if you are not, you really should understand the variables and know the vocabulary. If you are in a store and the sofa only comes "as is," take a good look at the following in order to decide if you like the sofa well enough to buy it and live with it for five or ten years. We typically review the following:

Cushion shape and fill. For each piece, decide on the type of cushion fill you desire and select a tight or a loose back for the cushions. Although some people prefer loose pillow-back sofas for the added comfort, tight backs and tufted backs are neater, especially when you add throw pillows into the equation. The seat cushions should be firmer than the back ones. An 86-inch sofa should always have three cushions, while a 6-foot sofa can have one or two. Some styles have square or rectangular seat cushions, but if the arms are set back, the cushions will wrap around them in a T-shape.

Arms. Arms can be scrolled with or without an inset panel. They may be slightly rolled over, or tailored and square. A lower, flat arm is generally more casual and easier to lie down on than a high, straight arm.

Legs. Visible legs can be of metal or wood, which may be turned or spooled, stained, gilded, or polished. Note that wood legs often need casters on front legs only, because if there are casters on the back legs, the piece will move when you sit down. Exposed legs are very airy and clean and allow the sofa to sit up off the floor.

Skirts. Decide what style of skirt is desired, if any. Inverted corner pleats, shirring, or a straight drop are some of the choices. A dressmaker's skirt drops softly down from the top of the platform (right under

the seat cushion) to the floor, giving you an elegant 12-inch-high skirt. A kick-pleat skirt starts a few inches below the platform with a rolled welt or some type of trim at the top. If you are using bullion as a skirt accent, we recommend 8-inch bullion. (Always specify either two rows of bullion or one row in front of the skirt.) Tape trim on a skirt is usually set up the width of the tape. Contrast binding is on the bottom of a skirt and can be ¾ inch to an inch.

Edge finishes. How should the seams on a piece be finished? Options include a self-welt, contrast binding, cord, or other trim. The upholsterer should be able to show you examples of each.

Tufting. Other details include tufting on the back or on the inside of the arms, with or without contrasting buttons. Tufting can be deep with buttons, or shallow with stitching only.

SLIPCOVERS

Slipcovers are not an alternative to your regular upholstery. You should only use them for a sort of "shabby chic" or beach-house look. They are not very practical. First, they can be expensive. Any piece you choose to slipcover will still have to be upholstered at least in sateen, so you are in effect paying twice. Slipcovers should be considered an extra, rather than a way to save money. Also, it is not practical to have different sets for winter and summer unless you have a lot of storage space, as well as someone to iron and steam out the wrinkles every season and then dress the furniture when the slipcovers are changed.

A practical use for slipcovers is to protect good upholstery. For example, if you have selected an expensive silk for your dining chairs, you might want some simple slipcovers to protect the seats from small

RIGHT:
This intimate sitting room has so many subtle details. The chair and matching rectangular ottoman are upholstered in a small-scale patterned cotton with double-inverted corner pleats. In contrast, the cushions on the wood frame chair are solid and smooth. This scheme carefully weaves open and closed furniture, sheer and opaque materials, and solids with patterns to create visual interest.

OPPOSITE:
The monochromatic palette of a Nantucket beach house is a calming one, with a variety of textured beige and cream cotton fabrics and a beige and cream Elizabeth Eakins rug. The sofas are slipcovered to maintain the casual look. The only accent color comes from the blue of the ocean and the sky.

children. (Or you could buy a few extra yards of the fabric from the dye lot you are using for the upholstery and put it away to reupholster the seats that become soiled.)

You might also use a slipcover if you have inherited or bought an antique chair or sofa with antique fabric or tapestry that you want to preserve. Covering it with a slipcover is a good way to protect your investment. But remember that you are also hiding the lines of the piece.

Slipcovers go in and out of style like the length of skirts. They make a statement and, like everything else that makes a statement, there is an art to it. They are available commercially and of course from upholsterers. If you decide to use slipcovers on your furniture, the whole look of the room should adopt a similarly casual and relaxed mood.

SELECTING APPROPRIATE FABRICS

Although not an exact science, identifying the right fabric for your chosen furniture forms does follow some universal guidelines. The following is a more specific discussion of the fabric fundamentals we established in Chapter 5, since the time has come for us to put that information to work.

COLOR. What is the chosen palette for the room where this piece of furniture will be placed? Think back to the colors of the rug you selected. You could pick one predominant color and one accent color from the rug and find a fabric to complement it. Or you could let the rug stand alone and choose one color from its palette to determine a monochromatic theme for the fabric. Ask yourself: Does this fabric fit

ADMITTEDLY, C&K HAS A LOVE AFFAIR WITH PILLOWS. YOU MIGHT EVEN SAY THAT WE ARE OBSESSED WITH THEM. FOR US, THEY ARE NOT AN AFTERTHOUGHT BUT AN INTEGRAL PART OF THE UPHOLSTERY PROCESS. FOR EXAMPLE, WHEN PLANNING THE UPHOLSTERY FOR A SOFA, WE SIMULTANEOUSLY DECIDE HOW MANY PILLOWS TO MAKE, AND WE CHOOSE THEIR FABRICS AND TRIM. THE REASONS FOR THE ALLURE OF PILLOWS ARE MANY. FIRST OF ALL, ACCENT PILLOWS MAKE FURNITURE APPEAR MORE INVITING AND COMFORTABLE; A COUCH WITHOUT PILLOWS LOOKS A BIT NAKED TO US. FROM A DECORATING STANDPOINT, THESE EYE-CATCHING LITTLE BITS OF PUNCTUATION AROUND A ROOM DISTRIBUTE FABRICS AND COLORS TO EMPHASIZE THE CENTRAL PALETTE. ACCENT PILLOWS ALSO ADD A LITTLE FUN TO YOUR INTERIORS. BECAUSE OF THEIR SIZE, ACCENT PILLOWS CAN BE MADE OF A VERY EXPENSIVE FABRIC OR A ONE-OF-A-KIND PIECE (SUCH AS AN ANTIQUE REMNANT) THAT COULD NOT BE USED FOR REGULAR UPHOLSTERY APPLICATIONS. FOR THE SAME REASON, YOU MIGHT BE MORE INCLINED TO LAVISH MORE EXPENSIVE TRIMS ON A PILLOW THAN YOU COULD ON THE MAIN UPHOLSTERED PIECES. ALTHOUGH ACCENT PILLOWS REALLY CAN BE MADE IN ANY SIZE, OUR STANDARDS ARE 13 BY 17 INCHES FOR A CLUB CHAIR PILLOW AND 18 INCHES SQUARE FOR PILLOWS ON A SOFA.

in or does it create a welcome contrast? Is it too strong or is it just the right anchor for the room? Is it the correct shade of the desired color? All the fabrics in a room should honor each other, rather than exist independently of one another or of the palette set forth by the rug in the room.

STYLE. As we wrote in Chapter 5, certain fabrics are inherently more suitable than others on certain types of furniture. Durability is one factor, but style is also very important. Some fabrics are more "correct" than others from a historical perspective if the piece of furniture is antique. For example, Hepplewhite or Sheraton chairs should be upholstered in a stripe or a small-scale woven fabric, rather than in damask with a large-scale pattern. Arts and Crafts–style furniture is appropriately upholstered in a small-scale or solid-woven fabric or in linen printed with a period design.

If your sofa should be dressed in woven silk to be historically correct, but you want it to be used by your children while they watch

RIGHT:

1. A 1920s vintage Fortuny striped tape has been mitered and sewn together, creating concentric squares on the pillow at the back. The front pillow has 18th-century Persian embroidery hand reapplied to ivory silk fabric and 18th-century metallic tape with a wavy edge that frames the pillow face.

2. The tassel trim on the back pillow is doubled and hand-sewn to show off the complicated heading. On the front pillow, 19th-century French fabric has been hand-embroidered. The cord is new.

3. The back pillow was hand-embroidered in Paris with two different-color metallic threads. On the front pillow, a late 19th-century French textile fragment was too small for a complete pillow, so we centered it in a cream silk under piped-in celadon and

framed it with a new flat metallic tape trim; the pillow is bordered with a luscious cut moss.

4. The tassel fringe on the back pillow is inset in the seams, which obscures the heading for a more restrained look. The front pillow was appliquéd with 19th-century French Empire silk, incorporating metallic grosgrain and multiple appliqué cords.

5. For the back pillow, a striped velvet was mitered and edged with a "caterpillar" trim—part loop, part cut edge. On the front pillow, the silk taffeta was hand-sewn with wide tape trim around the edges on both sides with mitered corners, in what we call the envelope style.

OPPOSITE:
The quintessential beach-house recipe—off-white, beige, and pale blue with a minimal pattern.

3.

1.

2.

4.

5.

television, either choose a different fabric or use a different sofa. To find the appropriate textile for an antique, look it up in a dictionary of historical styles. Be aware that if you have chosen a contemporary fabric for a traditional piece of furniture, the piece will no longer look historical. But it will look new—and fresh (which can be liberating!). Just make sure that your choice is an informed one, so that you get the look you want rather than an unfortunate mistake.

TEXTURE. The tactile aspects of a fabric can convey a mood, so as you choose a fabric, think about the feeling that you want it to evoke. For example, you might select a soft chenille for the sofa in a family room and a traditional silk damask for the sofa in a formal living room.

RELATIONSHIPS. As you choose fabric, be mindful of adjacency. Avoid having two variations on the same kind of fabric next to each other in a room. Again, the goal is to distribute your fabrics by color, pattern, and texture so that the room feels balanced and not too repetitive.

SELECTING APPROPRIATE TRIMS

Upholstery seams should be finished with some sort of trim or detail, not only for a decorative accent, but also because a blind seam left untrimmed can pull apart. Wherever there is a seam on a piece of upholstered furniture, you will have to decide how you want it to be seen. This can be as simple as a rolled edge made of the same fabric as the upholstery (known as a self welt), or it can be a rolled edge of a different fabric (known as a contrast welt). Or you could choose one of the many applied trims—plain, plaited, or crepe cording; a braid or gimp tape; or fringes, such as bullion, tassels, or balls. On some leather upholstery, such as a Jean-Michel Frank sofa, we do not specify welt or trim of any kind, preferring instead to see baseball stitching.

Although secondary to fabrics in their importance, trims offer creative options of their own. Use trim to emphasize the shape of a piece of furniture or to accent the seams of a cushion edge or skirt detail. A trim can have its own personality or be part of the whole. A contrasting trim will stand out, while a multicolor trim might blend in with the palette of the accompanying fabric.

The Upholsterer's Guide to Good Furniture

ONE OF OUR FAVORITE UPHOLSTERERS, JIMMY COGEMA, WAS KIND ENOUGH TO OFFER THE FOLLOWING INFORMATION ABOUT THE CONSTRUCTION OF GOOD FURNITURE, AND WE ARE PASSING IT ALONG WITH SOME TIPS OF OUR OWN.

FRAME. THE FRAME OF A SEATING PIECE SHOULD BE MADE OF A HARD WOOD, SUCH AS MAPLE. ALL JOINTS SHOULD BE DOWELED AND GLUED, WITH CORNER BLOCKS TO HOLD THE FRAME TOGETHER. THE CORNER BLOCKS SHOULD BE SCREWED—RATHER THAN STAPLED—INTO THE FRAME. THE BACK POSTS AND BACK LEGS OF THE FRAME SHOULD BE MADE IN ONE PIECE FOR STRENGTH.

FOUNDATION. THE FRAME OF THE SEAT SHOULD BE WEBBED. COIL SPRINGS ARE USED ON THE SEATS AND BACKS AND SHOULD BE HAND-SEWN IN PLACE (NOT STAPLED) AND HAND-TIED. THE SPRINGS ARE THEN COVERED WITH BURLAP AND SEWN TO PREVENT THE COILS FROM MOVING. ON THE BODY OF THE PIECE, ALL THE STITCH WORK SHOULD BE DONE BY HAND. FOR THE INSIDE OF THE FURNITURE, EITHER 100 PERCENT POLYESTER OR A COMBINATION OF HOG HAIR AND POLYESTER FIBERS IS USED. THIS IS CALLED DOUBLE STUFFING. BACKS AND ARMS ARE ALSO DOUBLE-STUFFED FOR SUPPORT AND STRENGTH, BUT SHOULD STILL BE SOFT ENOUGH FOR COMFORT. DOWN PADS ARE USED ON ARMS AND BACKS WHENEVER POSSIBLE. THE DOWN SHOULD BE 80 PERCENT GOOSE DOWN WITH 20 PERCENT FEATHERS. THIS IS VERY IMPORTANT FOR COMFORT. CUSHIONS CAN ALSO BE MADE OF 80/20 DOWN OR A COMBINATION OF FOAM AND DOWN. IF THE LATTER, THE FOAM CAN BE SOFT, MEDIUM, OR HARD, DEPENDING ON THE CLIENT'S WISHES. KEEP IN MIND THAT DOWN MUST BE FLUFFED, BECAUSE IT TENDS TO KEEP AN IMPRESSION AFTER SOMEONE SITS ON IT. SOMEONE WITH BACK PROBLEMS SHOULD CHOOSE A COMBINATION OF FOAM AND DOWN.

COVER. THE FABRIC SHOULD BE CUT SO THAT THERE ARE PERFECT MATCHES. IF THE CLIENT HAS CHOSEN A HEAVY FABRIC, IT SHOULD BE CUT SO THAT THE INVERTED CORNER PLEATS LIE FLAT. TACKS SHOULD BE USED TO HOLD THE FABRIC IN PLACE RATHER THAN STAPLES, BECAUSE IF THE PIECE OF FURNITURE IS EVER RE-COVERED, REMOVING STAPLES WILL ALSO REMOVE PARTS OF THE FRAME.

RIGHT:
Because comfort was the driving force in the upholstery decisions for this Greenwich, Connecticut, library/family room, we chose club chairs with loose pillow backs.

OPPOSITE:
Antique chairs can look modern and sculptural when upholstered in solid fabrics with streamlined details. Here the simple cord and gimp on this pair of Biedermeier chairs matches the main fabric and emphasizes the wood inlay and metal ornamentation of the chairs.

Working with an Upholsterer

If you plan to work with an upholsterer, you should understand that some upholsterers will only work to the trade, meaning that they deal only with professional decorators or designers. Once you find an upholsterer, either through word of mouth or advertisement, we recommend that you carefully read the section below and be prepared to ask a lot of questions.

A good upholsterer can help you refine your vision before you make a commitment to specific pieces of furniture. There is a wealth of information and inspiration in an upholsterer's showroom or studio, including furniture forms upholstered in plain muslin. Because they are not covered with any specific fabric, you will not be swayed by a particular color or pattern and can focus solely on the silhouette before you decide whether or not you like it. With luck, you can rearrange the showroom pieces to simulate your room and to experiment with different layouts. Some workrooms will even let you borrow the muslin forms to try them out in your own space.

Once you find a few forms that appeal to you visually, sit in them to determine whether or not you like the comfort. Then pay attention to the depth of the seat, the tilt of the back, the height of the arm. Remember, too, that other members of your family will be sitting in the furniture, and take into consideration what their needs might be in terms of height and back support. A person 5 feet tall may find one type of seat comfortable, whereas someone who is 6 feet, 6 inches tall will prefer a seat in different proportions. A good upholsterer can adjust the depth, height, and width of a piece if necessary.

PRICING AND ORDERING. In order to receive exactly what you expect, there are many specifics that must be clearly and thoroughly communicated with your upholsterer. This is best done in writing, by means of your purchase order. This same degree of specification is required for every single piece in every room.

DIMENSIONS. Your purchase order should reconfirm the length, the width, and the height of every piece, especially if there have been any changes to the design along the way. Remember that the depth of the chair is not always its footprint. The measurement is best taken when a piece is pushed up against a wall, because there is always a slight slant to the back.

FABRIC GUIDELINES. The furniture dimensions you provide constitute essential information that will help your upholsterer determine how much yardage is required. As discussed in Chapter 5, you will also need to give the upholsterer the width of your fabric, as well as the repeat and drop of the pattern (if any), and the direction of the pattern, so that the upholsterer can tell you exactly how much fabric you need. This is the upholsterer's responsibility, not yours.

We recommend cutting a fabric swatch and stapling it to the purchase order with the correct side facing up and in the correct direction and position. In our experience, however, sometimes even this precaution is not enough. Many years ago, we ordered a large quantity of fabric and sent some yardage to our upholsterer and some to our curtain maker. We attached a swatch of the fabric to both purchase orders, with the "right" side of the fabric indicated on each. Unbeknownst to us, the fabric house had mislabeled the showroom sample, and we had indicated the "wrong" side of the fabric on our purchase orders! Our curtain maker decided to ignore our purchase order and use the reverse (in this case, correct) side of the fabric. Unfortunately, the upholsterer did the opposite and followed our directions, and we ended up with the curtains showing one side of the fabric and the upholstery showing the other. Lesson learned: You can never check or recheck often enough.

COST. Custom upholstery work is costly, so be sure you understand the pricing and how much you are spending on any given piece. Reconfirm the cost with your upholsterer if any changes are made (either to the furniture form or the fabric), and also inquire about any additional costs for special requests, finishes, rush work, and so on.

FINAL CONFIRMATION. Remember that once you order a piece of furniture and fabric for the upholstery, they are yours. No one wants a piece of beautiful furniture to arrive completed, only to find unexpectedly that it cannot be used. Before you place your final order, be sure to double-check crucial logistical information. Will the piece fit into your elevator? Through the doorway? Down the hallway? Around the corner? Is its final location still in accordance with your floor plan? With regard to the fabric, what is the lead time for completion of a piece after the upholsterer receives the fabric and trim? How does this fit in with your required installation goals? Also, as a final checkpoint for correct fabric usage and direction, visit your upholsterer to review your fabric after it arrives from the mill and before he or she starts to work on your piece.

Will the upholsterer confirm the amount of fabric you need? How does the firm accept payment—cash or credit card? Is a deposit required and is the balance due before delivery? Can you come to the showroom to see the work in progress or to check on it before final delivery? Will the upholsterer order the frame before receiving all of your fabric—or wait for the fabric and then order the frame?

MAKING A BED THE CULLMAN & KRAVIS WAY

Although not technically upholstery, the linens you choose for your bedding are akin to the fabrics you choose for your furniture and should be considered with the same care. Walk into any fine linens shop, and you will be astounded by the range of choices: pillows in many different shapes and sizes; different covers for blankets, duvets; coverlets and the like—not to mention the dozens of color and fabric options. Our clients often ask us which pieces they should buy. So as part of our down-to-the-very-last detail service for clients, we use the following guidelines for a stylishly made bed in the Cullman & Kravis way.

King-size bed: 3 European (square) shams; 3 standard shams; 2 boudoir pillows shams (optional), 1 blanket cover; 1 duvet cover

Queen-size bed: 2 European (square) shams, 2 standard shams, 2 boudoir pillows shams (optional), 1 blanket cover, 1 duvet cover

Twin-size bed: 1 king-size sham, 1 standard sham, 1 boudoir pillow sham (optional), 1 blanket cover, 1 duvet cover

We make a bed with the European shams next to the headboard, then the standard shams, then the boudoir pillows. We rarely use a pillowcase because the design is typically only on one side of the pillow

OPPOSITE:
Paley sofas are a great choice when sofas float in the middle of a room, because they have a scroll back and a low, unobtrusive arm.

LEFT:
The dramatic four-poster bed, with its bold mahogany turnings, is the centerpiece of this Hamptons master bedroom/sitting room suite. The linens are embroidered with a stylized wave pattern, and the box spring is upholstered in a soft check. One of our most popular upholstery forms is the double chaise, seen in the sitting room beyond the master bedroom. Measuring 5 feet square, it is ideal for two people to read or watch television with their feet up.

BELOW LEFT:
This mattress-ticking headboard is highly tailored in a refined country style. The shaped corner, contrast welt, and inset frame are sophisticated details.

BELOW RIGHT:
The headboard with its shirred border is upholstered in the same printed silk as the walls. The bed linens and a hand-woven bed throw reinforce the cream-and-gold color scheme.

rather than all around, as on shams. Some clients prefer to store the pillows they actually sleep on in a closet, swapping them with all the shams at bedtime. This process allows the bed to look fresh and pristine when not being used. If you choose to keep these pillows on the bed instead of in the closet, we recommend putting them between the European shams and the standard shams. The bed should be made with a thin blanket over the top sheet and then a blanket cover tucked in. At the foot of the bed, we fold the duvet in thirds.

Bed-linen Design

White sheets with colored embroidery threads are always classic and elegant. Although these sheets are available commercially, even in catalogues, we prefer custom embroidery, for which we choose a design and thread colors to complement other fabrics in the room. Many retailers of fine linens will work with you on a custom design. Some have thousands of designs in stock. However, if you bring in a fabric or a picture or even

an architectural element that you like, they will create a design just for you. Beyond embroidery, you might wish to customize bed linens with hemstitching between the sheet cuff and the sheet, a 4-inch linen cuff or bordered edge, a curlicue floral monogram, or scalloping. Like any custom goods, these special linens are expensive and not returnable, so be sure you order exactly what you want. A further point: Be sure to clear all custom choices with your partner or your teenager from the perspective of texture and color. It would be a shame if the person actually sleeping on the bedding did not like it. If custom embroidery is not possible, there are many ready-made embroidered sheets. You can even have simple percale sheets embroidered inexpensively.

Our preference is for everything in a sheet set to be embroidered in the same style and color to give the bed a visual consistency. You should probably have three sets in total. That was the traditional thinking for a bridal trousseau: one set on the bed, one set in the wash, and one spare set in the cupboard, in case of an emergency. The sets can, of course, be different, but we do not recommend mixing up the sets on the bed. To economize, European shams and blanket covers could be plain white piqué or diamond matelassé, which will complement the different sheet sets. Boudoir pillows should match the sets. Also, the duvet cover could be plain and possibly coordinate with more than one set. If there is not enough of the primary fabric present in a bedroom, you can make the European shams of that material, but not if it is the same material as on the upholstered headboard.

Headboards and Mattresses

Although we sometimes fall in love with antique wooden beds, there is no denying that upholstered headboards are more comfortable. We like the fabric and trim on the headboard and the dust ruffle to match. All Cullman & Kravis upholstered headboards are generally 27 inches higher than the top of the mattress, so that the overall height is approximately 51 inches if you use a standard 24-inch-high mattress. Be sure to indicate to your upholsterer the height of the box spring as well.

We prefer a 24-inch-high mattress because 21-inch mattresses are too low and 27-inch mattresses are too high in relation to night tables. Aesthetically, we like our beds higher to keep in scale with the room and the architecture. The measurements of a 7-inch mattress and 17-inch bed skirt create a nice proportion, although recently many people have chosen very tall mattresses—often 11 to 13 inches thick—which has created an aesthetic challenge. To stay in scale, we have been making taller headboards and slightly higher night tables.

Case Study:

Ellie's living room in Stamford, Connecticut, has a warmly inviting ambience, thanks to the careful selection of forms and fabrics, all of which complement her collection of Americana. The two C&K sofas sitting at right angles to each other have tight backs and are upholstered in red-and-green plaid with multicolor bullion; the ottoman has a matching fabric with a pleated skirt and a tufted top with buttons. The Odom chair at the left near the sofa is covered in a solid green fabric and has a lightly shirred skirt. In the foreground, the leather-covered sofa is flanked by a "personality" chair at the left—a small, antique Napoleon III painted chair with spool work, a simple upholstered seat with nail

heads—and by an authentic period wooden chair at the right with a tufted suede seat with buttons.

Accessory fabrics are used on the pillows and throws. On the C&K sofas, the back pillows with knife edges are solid, and the front pillows, also knife edge, are covered in the same fabric as that of the curtains, which picks up a floral pattern similar to the design of the rug. A woven cashmere throw rests on the arm of the Odom chair, and an antique quilt is draped over the back of the leather sofa. The pillows on this sofa have Turkish corners with loop fringe.

Chapter 7: The Windows

A ROOM WITHOUT FABRIC ON THE WINDOWS IS LIKE A SOFA
WITHOUT PILLOWS—NAKED AND INCOMPLETE. CURTAINS
EMBODY OUR OBSESSION WITH FORM AND FUNCTION. WE
CHOOSE CURTAIN STYLES BASED ON THE PRACTICAL NEEDS OF
A PARTICULAR ROOM, TAKING INTO ACCOUNT THE DECORATING
STYLE OF THE ROOM AND OF THE HOUSE AS A WHOLE. CURTAINS
"MULTITASK"—NOT ONLY DO THEY SERVE AS IMPORTANT DESIGN
STATEMENTS, BUT THEY ALSO PROVIDE PRIVACY AND BLOCK
THE SUN. THE ARTISTRY IS IN THE SELECTION OF THE FABRIC,
AND THE NUANCE IS IN HOW IT IS EDGED, LINED, INTERLINED,
AND INSTALLED, WITH SUCH DETAILS AS TAPE AND TASSELS,
CONTRAST FABRIC, CUFFS, AND DECORATIVE HARDWARE. A
WELL-DESIGNED CURTAIN SETS A MOOD BY CREATING ILLU-
SIONS WITH LIGHT AND AIR.

OPPOSITE:
In a South Carolina beach
house, we used unlined linen
curtains with a French
heading mounted on a simple
bronze pole. The untrimmed
curtains are embroidered
with a whimsical, custom,
leaf-shape design.

The C&K Way: Curtain Fringe Placement.

IF YOU WANT YOUR CURTAINS TO HAVE TASSEL FRINGE RUNNING DOWN THE
FRONTS AND ACROSS THE BOTTOM EDGES OF THE PANELS, AND IF YOU WANT
YOUR CURTAINS TO PUDDLE ON THE FLOOR, THE TRIM HEADING CANNOT BE
CONCEALED. INSTEAD, THE TRIM SHOULD BE SEWN ON THE BOTTOM EDGE OF
THE CURTAIN SET UP THE WIDTH OF THE TRIM SO THAT THE TASSELS DO
NOT SIT ON THE FLOOR BUT ON THE FABRIC. DOWN THE FRONT EDGES, THE
HEADING CAN BE SEWN AT THE EDGE, ALLOWING THE TASSELS TO DANGLE, OR
THEY CAN BE SEWN SET IN THE WIDTH OF THE TRIM, JUST AS IT IS ON THE
BOTTOM, ALLOWING THE TASSELS TO DANGLE IN FRONT OF A CUFF OF FABRIC.
BE SURE THE HEADING IS SYMPATHETIC IN BOTH COLOR AND DESIGN TO THE
MAIN CURTAIN FABRIC.

FORM FOLLOWS FUNCTION

In curtain designs, we decide first what the window coverings should
accomplish in every room. We begin with the most important rooms—
living room, dining room, master bedroom—and then move on to
secondary rooms, keeping in mind where the windows are located in
each room and what is happening outside those windows. To help
assemble a plan for your window treatments, think about your needs
in regard to the following issues.

PRIVACY CONCERNS. What do you see through the window when
looking in from the outside? Is the window at street level, or does it face
directly into the home of your neighbors (and vice versa)? Bedrooms,
bathrooms, and dressing rooms, of course, have different privacy issues
than a kitchen or a family room. In urban settings, windows in almost
every room often require some degree of privacy control. A small powder room on the ground level in the suburbs might need only a café
curtain on the bottom half of the window, whereas a powder room in
the city might call for complete coverage. To design curtains that "work,"
you must fully understand what your windows require if they are to
solve your privacy needs.

CONTROL OF LIGHT. Look at the direction the window faces and
note how much light comes through, not just in the morning but at
other times of the day. For example, in a bedroom with a window that
faces east, you might need to block out light in the morning but allow
light in freely during the daytime, while simultaneously providing
privacy. Rooms containing fine art or antiques will also need a degree
of light control.

In a living room facing west, the furniture might need protection
against afternoon sun, which can be very strong and produce a good
deal of heat.

VIEW ENHANCEMENT (OR CONCEALMENT). Do not be afraid
to lose a beautiful view by covering it with curtains. On the contrary,
eye-catching curtains that are drawn open will soften the edge of the
window frame and highlight a beloved view. On the other hand, some
scenes may need to be camouflaged, particularly in urban settings where
the view may be of an airshaft or a brick wall. In these instances, the
most appropriate window covering is a scrim or a frosted-glass window.

DECORATING STATEMENTS. By now you should have established
a hierarchy for your rooms. Public spaces that are frequented by guests
and used for entertaining, such as the living room and the dining room,
need windows that make a statement. In these rooms, the curtains are
there to be seen and admired. Important private rooms, such as the master
bedroom and the library, should command a similar, distinctive presence through their curtains. Less important or elaborate curtains can be
reserved for such locations as the home office or breakfast room or hallway.

Form Follows Form

Given the importance we place on architecture in Chapter 3, we believe in a strong relationship between the form of the actual window and the form of the curtains. As you analyze the style, shape, and proportion of your windows, you will realize that only certain curtains will work with certain windows.

STYLES. The style of your curtains should be in harmony with the overall style of your house. Think of the adjectives that apply to the architectural style of your home (and, we hope, of your windows as well), be it traditional or contemporary, urban or country. Then further classify your windows within their particular style as formal or casual. For example, a Colonial-style house would look strange with windows dressed in deep valances and heavy curtains, which would dwarf the simple lines of the rooms and add too much visual weight overhead. Even when we design traditional-style curtains, they may be full, but they are never heavy. We try to make them as light as possible because curtains should never induce claustrophobia.

Well-designed window coverings are composed of different elements, which depend on your personal preferences and needs. Some treatments are simple—such as a sheer café curtain or a plain valance on a kitchen window. Others are more complex. For example, a bedroom window may require three layers of material: a decorative curtain to dress the window, a sheer scrim of fabric for privacy, and a blackout shade to control the light. Curtain styles are such a huge topic that it would be impossible to describe everything in this chapter. See the Bibliography for additional information on this subject.

SHAPES. What do your windows look like? Most windows are rectangles, for which there are many curtain options. But exceptions such as bay windows may need more complicated design solutions. Are they round or arched? Flat or curved? Consider the height and width of your windows. Are they especially tall or wide? Do not forget the relationship of windows to walls and number of windows in the room, because a group of windows lined up on a wall looks quite different than a single one positioned in the center of a wall.

LENGTH. Curtains are all about lengths and widths. We always recommend long curtains unless there is some good reason not to have them, such as a window seat or a built-in bookcase under a window. Mount curtains above and outside the window trim on both sides, even all the way up to the crown, in order to elongate the ceiling height, and

In this master bedroom, a double swag is installed on a reeded mahogany pole with finials. Note how the striped fabric is sewn in the opposite direction of the swag, so that the fabric for the valance and the panels can run in the same direction. The curtains are lined and interlined for a fuller effect.

LEFT:
Full-height café curtains are installed inside the trim in this Long Island beach house. Although it is often tempting to leave a small window alone, unlined airy sheers like these are simple and to the point, focusing one's eyes on the view and providing a welcome softness at the window, especially at night.

ABOVE:
Tableau curtains describe panels that are made to draw at the top of the window. These are shirred over the pole with no visible hardware, perfect for this peacefully sophisticated Manhattan bedroom.

Because the reverse side of the curtains is visible with this treatment, we used a coordinating fabric for the contrast lining. As always, we avoided using silk on the side of the curtain that faces the sun because silk is not stable when exposed to sunlight.

as far as 6 to 8 inches out on either side of the trim. Curtains should not end above the floor. That makes them look as if they have outgrown the windows. Instead, allow them to end in a 2-inch break if they have no trim. With trim, the break can equal the height of the trim.

When there is a window seat or some kind of cabinetry beneath a window, the curtains cannot hang to the floor. Instead, extend a pair of short curtains down to just below the sill. There are two main types of short curtains. The first type hangs from the top of the window to the sill, generally in panel pairs that can be drawn open or closed. We typically use these over a window seat in a room where this is the only window in the room, or where there are full-length curtain panels on the other windows. The second type, known as a café curtain, usually covers only half the window and is very casual looking. It is appropriate for windows where some privacy is desired, but where light and view are important, as in a powder room or a kitchen. We prefer café curtains that are sheer rather than opaque, because a café curtain in a heavy fabric looks clumsy. Ideally, cafés look loose, light, and airy.

WIDTH. Curtain width is about fullness. When curtain makers speak of width, they refer to the number of widths of fabric in the curtain panel. When you look at a curtain, the panels, whether they are long or short, should look ample and full when the curtains are open, and not too skimpy or stretched when they are closed. If the curtains are not designed to be drawn, the panels should still look as if they could be closed.

Here is the formula for figuring out the width of your panels: Your goal is to have a panel with double or 100 percent fullness. This means that on a window 8 feet wide, each panel will have to close across a width of about 4 feet. If you want double fullness in each panel, you will need 8 feet of fabric in each panel, which is almost two widths of a standard 54-inch-wide fabric.

To draw or not to draw? We prefer not to have our curtains draw across the window, because we do not want to ruin the careful folds created by the curtain maker. In fact, we often have the installer mount a small loop from the baseboard to a hidden hook on the curtains so they cannot be moved by mistake.

If two windows are next to each other, you can create the illusion of one large composition with three curtain panels, or three panels on a rod. This means that the center panel closes across half of each window plus the wall space and trim between the two windows, leaving only a quarter of the window for the remaining side panels to cover. For example, on two adjacent 4-foot windows with 10 inches of wall space between them and the curtain rod extending 6 inches beyond the side of each window, there is a total of about 10 feet to cover. The side panels then have to cover 2 ½ feet each, and the center panel has to close over 5 feet. In order to calculate the fullness, double these measurements. However, if the panels are not supposed to close, you could take out some of the fullness to keep them looking light and airy. On a very wide expanse that cannot have an extra pair of curtains in the middle—French doors, for example—we do not really want them to close because they would look too full. Given all these scenarios and nuances, you will be wise to work with a professional curtain maker.

LOGISTICS. Consider the usage of both the window and the curtains. How does the window open? How does this impact the curtains and vice versa? Pay attention to your ventilation systems. Is there a radiator protruding from under the windowsill for a few feet or for the whole length of the window? Also note the location of floor grilles. If they are close to where your planned curtains would stack or puddle, you must choose a substantial curtain fabric, or else tack down or weight the edges of the curtain panels so they do not move in the breeze of your heat or air-conditioning. Better yet, guard against this prior to construction by placing floor vents where the curtain panel will not fall.

VALANCES

Window treatments are about more than just curtains. To finish our windows, we also use valances and shades, sometimes with curtains and sometimes without. Valances are decorative coverings at the top of a window frame. Certain styles of valances are always paired with curtain

OPPOSITE:
This is a typical elevation of French doors with a pair of windows on either side where the panels are stationary; the curtains are never meant to actually close across the window. We have used one pair of stationary curtain panels at the windows and another pair flanking the doors. The inside pair is double width and would cover the windows if pulled. The fabric is unlined white linen embroidered with a multicolor curvilinear vine design. The curtains are mounted on wood poles with rings and small finials and trimmed with a jute cord that is hand sewn to the fronts and bottoms of the curtains.

LEFT:
A shirred shaped valance is a soft, feminine treatment for a master bedroom. If you have a favorite fabric, highlight it by using it more than once. Here the blue-and-white hand-printed cotton is used on both the bedskirt and the curtains.

FRENCH DOORS, WHICH ARE WIDELY USED IN NON-URBAN SETTINGS, ARE ALWAYS A SOURCE OF CONSTERNATION FOR US FROM THE CURTAIN STANDPOINT. TYPICALLY, THE GLASS DOORS OPEN INTO THE ROOM AND THE SCREENS OPEN OUT, WHICH CREATES A DILEMMA IF YOU WANT BOTH VENTILATION AND LIGHT CONTROL. WHEN THE DOORS BOTH OPEN, THEY ALWAYS CATCH THE CURTAINS. THE SHADE IS ON THE INSIDE OF THE ROOM, OF COURSE, BUT IT CANNOT BE MOUNTED ABOVE THE DOOR, BECAUSE THEN THE DOOR CANNOT BE OPENED WHEN THE SHADE IS DOWN. IF A SHADE IS MOUNTED ON THE DOOR, THE BRACKET WILL BE VISIBLE BECAUSE YOU CANNOT HIDE IT WITH A CURTAIN AND LIGHT WILL LEAK AROUND THE EDGES. IT IS ALSO QUITE CHALLENGING TO DRESS A PAIR OF DOORS THAT OPEN WITH A DOUBLE-WIDE MULLION BETWEEN THEM. A BETTER CURTAIN SCENARIO IS TO HAVE ONLY ONE OPERATING DOOR FLANKED BY TWO STATIONARY SIDE PANELS OF GLASS OVER WHICH THE CURTAINS CAN HANG AND NOT BE TRAPPED AS THE DOORS OPEN AND CLOSE.

panels, whereas others can stand alone. A valance can be very ornate and elaborate—requiring additional labor, fabric, and trim—or it can be simple.

Like curtains, valances are described by length, width, and the type of heading. Like curtains also, the artistry is in the details of the construction, the fabric, and the integration into the design of the room. Valances can attach to the wall with visible decorative hardware such as rings and a pole or brackets and finials, which can be made of metal, such as bronze, or of stained, painted, or gilded wood. Valances may also be mounted on a dust board—a piece of plywood that you do not see when the curtain is installed. A dust board draws a harder line at the top of the valance that lets you see a straight line of fabric across the window while concealing the hardware.

Headings for Curtains and Valances

"Heading" is the term used to describe the way in which the top of the curtain fabric or valance attaches to the hardware. The different types of headings are often given different names, so we have included a few drawings with descriptions. All types of curtain headings can also be used for valance headings, and all valances can work with or without curtains beneath.

French rollback. When we specify a valance with curtains underneath, the valance gets the decorative heading while the underlying curtain panels have a simple, flat, pleated heading called a French rollback. A rollback has more fullness at the top of the pleat, so that the fold of the curtain is significant enough to retain its shape as it emerges from underneath the valance.

Pleated headings. Headings with three pleats or one pleat are often referred to as Brisbee headings. Other pleated headings include a classic French heading, which has three pleats pinched down. A side-pleated heading on rings is a simple and elegant look that works particularly well, because it looks as if the pleat were hanging down off the ring. A C&K tip is to emphasize one color of a stripe and use it for the center of a pinch pleat, so that it will not be lost in the folds of the pleat. Side-pleated headings are tailored and neat. They work very well in libraries, studies, and bedrooms, especially in plaids and prints. Sometimes, the pleats are rounded. This is called a goblet heading and is another of our favorite looks for a more formal interior. It works either as a heading for a valance or as a heading for curtains. A goblet heading can be made with rings or on a track with a cord and knots.

OPPOSITE:
Because there is very little room on either side of the windows in this Hamptons house, we chose the skinniest metal poles with rounded returns. Rounded returns take less space on the wall than finials do. F͟ understated look, curtains are unli͟ untrimmed, and the curtain hardware matches the finish on the door hardware.

LEFT:
Swags and jabots can be informal when used with a bamboo pole and finials. As always, "God is in the details." Here a decorative cord is draped over the swags and the bottom edges are trimmed with a decorative fringe. Half café curtains provide privacy from the terrace outside.

Shirred headings. This type is relatively feminine and appropriate for a bedroom or a bathroom, rather than for a more formal living or dining room. A shirred plaid or floral pattern may be a good option for a kitchen. A shirred valance should not have a large-scale repeat fabric, because you will lose the pattern in the shirring where the fabric is all above your head. We like to trim shirred headings with welts or cords and contrast stitching. For different effects, try varying the height of the piece above the shirring

Tab tops. These are informal curtain headings, often with contrast buttons or playful stitching, typically used in country houses and relatively informal areas of any house, such as the kitchen.

Swags and jabots. A swag is a panel of fabric that is draped horizontally on a dust board or over a pole, and a jabot is the tail that hangs down on the side. Swags and jabots can be used anywhere, with or without curtains underneath. The finished look of these window accents will depend on how they are mounted. Swags and jabots mounted on an exposed pole are light and airy and somewhat informal. Mounted on a dust board, the look is more formal, particularly if they have a central swag.

Determining the length of a jabot and the depth of the swag takes a lot of experience and flexibility, as well as imagination and skill. A good rule of thumb is to let the point of the fabric of the jabot line up with a pane of glass. You can also figure that the depth of any valence, especially swags, should take up about one-sixth to one-seventh the distance from floor to ceiling—or the same proportion as the head to the body of a human figure.

The length and look of a jabot are all about proportion and its impact on the look of the curtain. Do not forget to add contrast lining to swags and jabots and shirred valances, or to self-line them. This is critical, because when the fabric turns in a swag or swings out in shirring, a bit of the reverse side will always be visible.

SHADES
Window shades work in conjunction with curtains and sometimes instead of them.

Roman shades. A true Roman shade is flat and structured with a flap on the bottom. A rod is set in the bottom flap to keep the edge straight (see drawing). Our favorite method of light control is a Roman shade of sheer fabric, made without the bottom flap, allowing the bottom and the sides to droop down for a soft unstructured look. This provides moderate coverage for privacy yet still allows light into the room.

Balloon shades. Typically softer and fuller than Roman shades, they can be pleated across the top to look relatively tailored, or shirred across for a lush, opulent look.

Simple roller shades. Practical and easy to use, these are always appropriate for complete blackout, and we usually position them behind other window treatments, particularly in bedrooms. During the day, they can be rolled up and out of sight. For a more appealing look when rolled down, we have them laminated with a simple fabric. If you have enough room in the soffit over your windows, the ultimate convenience is a motorized shade.

Sheer or Solar weave shades. These are another option, but take care to consider the openness of the weave, since it will affect the amount of light and privacy in a room. Structured as shades (as opposed to curtains) with pull cords and a metal heading, and so on, sheer weave shades are great for UV protection, light control, and some privacy.

CURTAIN HARDWARE
Curtain hardware is the system that keeps curtains on the window. There is always hardware that is not visible—the nuts and bolts and brackets that the upholsterer uses to make sure the curtains are mounted properly. Our concern here is with the visible hardware. Should it make a decorative statement along with elaborate curtains, or should it fade into the background and let the curtain fabric and trim take center stage? To choose wisely, simply remember that up to this point, you have made many decisions about how you want your rooms to look, and window hardware should be in keeping with these goals.

The Hardware System, Design and Materials
The style of the hardware system should relate to the style and design of your home, the room, and the window. Select the style of the pole or rod first, and this will set the tone for the style of the accessories. Poles and rods with a clean, smooth design will work in any classic or contemporary interior, whereas more decorative designs, such as reeded or fluted poles and rods, are best in formal or urban settings.

Window hardware is usually made from wood or metal. Wood can be painted, stained, or gilded, and metal comes in a variety of finishes. Gilding and other metallic finishes add a bit of shine near the ceiling, which is always welcome, whereas a stained wooden pole looks rich and traditional. Choose the material and finish for your poles or rods first, followed by accessories such as brackets, rings, finials, and tiebacks.

Whatever style you decide upon, all the elements should match in terms of material, finish, and design. A professional curtain installer or upholster can offer some guidance as to which elements will be most suitable for your curtain selection.

Poles and brackets. Determine the length of pole required to span the window. We like the pole to extend about 6 inches on either side of the trim, so the curtain stack does not cover too much of the window itself. To choose a diameter for the pole, consider the scale of the room and the height of the ceiling. For example, if your room has a 9-foot ceiling, you should choose a diameter bigger than 1 ½ inches, or else the pole

LEFT:

It is easy to become enthusiastic about the beauty of curtain trims, which we apply down the front and bottom edges of curtains. There are so many different types, including tassels, loops, balls, and beads of fabric, wood, and crystal. Ask your upholsterer to have the trim sewn to the edge of the panel and let the detail of the heading show, as it does here. If you choose a simple tape, set it in off the edge by the width of the tape.

ABOVE:

The windows in this guest bedroom have three levels of window treatments—simple swags and jabots for decorative impact, unstructured sheer Roman shades for privacy, and blackout shades (not visible) beneath for light control. Because the room was so small, we decided to use the same fabric on the walls as on the windows in order to expand the visual perception of the room.

will look lost and unimportant in the scale of the room. Brackets supporting the pole are mounted on either the window molding or the wall. In new construction, be sure to add wooden blocking to prevent the brackets from coming out of the walls. The pole is mounted inside the trim only for a café curtain and does not extend past the trim.

Rings. Rings attach the curtain to the pole. The preferred method is with tiny hooks that are sewn onto the curtains. Your upholsterer or curtain maker will attach the appropriate number of rings to your curtains at correct intervals.

Finials. Finials are found at each end of a pole or rod and can be ornate (a carved shape) or simple (a plain ball or cap). Some poles and rods are sold with accompanying finials, and some offer a choice of design. We make our decision based on the size we need (a tiny finial, for instance, would disappear in a big room), or a favorite motif, such as an acorn or a pineapple. If one end of a pole is very close to the wall, it may not even need a finial on that side.

Tiebacks. Tiebacks are an added detail, if you like curtains that are held open. The curtains are simply draped behind the tiebacks, which are mounted to the wall. They are typically made from metal, fabrics, cord, or oversize tassels attached to cords.

RIGHT TOP:
A variation on the saw-toothed valance design, this valance is custom shaped to reference the Gothic crown molding. The edges of the points and the horizontal line of the top of the valance are bound with a welt of contrast fabric that ties the valance to the wall color. The same contrast fabric peeks out from beneath the points, echoing and reinforcing the pointed shape.

RIGHT BOTTOM:
A crisp Roman shade with inset contrast tape was used in this gentleman's dressing room-cum-study. When trimming a Roman shade, run the trim down both sides and across the bottom, in a U-shape.

BLOCKING OUT LIGHT COMPLETELY IN A ROOM, OR CREATING A BLACKOUT, CAN BE ACCOMPLISHED IN A COUPLE OF DIFFERENT WAYS BESIDES A ROLLER SHADE. FABRIC CURTAINS CAN BE FITTED WITH A BLACKOUT INTERLINING, ALTHOUGH THIS MAY CREATE A PROBLEM WITH SOME AIR-CONDITIONING SYSTEMS. IF YOU RELY ON LONG CURTAINS TO BLOCK OUT THE LIGHT, THEY WILL BE DRAWN IN FRONT OF THE AIR VENT AS WELL AS THE WINDOW. IT IS BEST IF THE CURTAINS CANNOT BE DRAWN, IN WHICH CASE A BLACKOUT SHADE TO THE SILL, POSITIONED INDEPENDENTLY BEHIND THE CURTAINS, WILL DO THE TRICK. SIMPLE VENETIAN BLINDS ARE YET ANOTHER OPTION. THEY PROVIDE ALMOST COMPLETE BLACKOUT, AND THEY ALSO ADDRESS PRIVACY NEEDS. IN BEDROOMS, YOUNG CHILDREN'S ROOMS, AND TELEVISION-VIEWING AREAS, VENETIAN BLINDS PROVIDE GOOD COVERAGE AND ARE THE MOST FUNCTIONAL WAY TO REGULATE NATURAL LIGHT AND STILL PRESERVE THE VIEW.

The C&K Way: The Allure of the Double-Hung Window.

DOUBLE-HUNG WINDOWS ALLOW FOR COMPLETE FLEXIBILITY OF CURTAIN DESIGN. WITH A DOUBLE-HUNG WINDOW, YOU AVOID THE PROBLEM OF FRENCH DOORS AND TILT-AND-TURN WINDOWS, WHERE THE FABRIC CAN GET CAUGHT WHEN THE DOORS OR WINDOWS ARE OPERATED. YOU CAN EASILY MOUNT A SHADE OF ANY TYPE ON A DOUBLE-HUNG WINDOW, EITHER WITHIN THE WINDOW OPENING OR ABOVE IT, UNDER A VALANCE OR BEHIND A CURTAIN ROD. IF YOU WANT OPTIMUM LIGHT CONTROL OR TOTAL BLACKOUT FROM YOUR SHADES, MOUNT THE SHADE OUTSIDE THE WINDOW OPENING AND COVER THE EDGES WITH THE CURTAINS TO CONTROL ALL THE LIGHT.

LEFT TOP:
Balloon shades don't have to be puffy or fussy. Here is a one-swag balloon shade, with two pleats instead of shirring and a bead trim.

LEFT BOTTOM:
This treatment is called "thrown over a pole." In this scenario, a swag without a jabot is installed with coordinating panels, one mounted over the swag and one underneath, creating the illusion that the fabric was casually draped over the pole. Since the curtains are stationary, a Venetian blind is used for privacy and light control.

ABOVE:
Sometimes we choose to have no visible window treatment, as in this informal Connecticut family room.

Installation

Curtain and hardware installations are not do-it-yourself projects and are best entrusted to an upholsterer. There are too many critical issues to consider—such as drilling into woodwork and wall. And, in the end, you do not want the curtains to fall down! Brackets have to be mounted correctly in the proper location, and poles should be at the right height for the curtains to hang properly. For windows wider than 4 feet, you may need support brackets mounted at the center of the window below the crown molding to prevent the rod from bowing.

FABRIC SELECTION

Your choice of fabric will have just as much impact on the curtain's overall effect as the design does, because the color will be distributed around the room in a major way. Remember when you are looking at curtains in your elevations, you should envision them as a mass of color and pattern against the wall, not just as a lifeless line drawing.

Try your fabric both in the morning and again at night with the lights on to confirm whether or not it can be seen through, to determine whether you will need some kind of blackout shade underneath. Also, some fabrics look beautiful during the day with natural light but can go dead in artificial light.

If you plan to use multiple elements for your window, such as curtain panels paired with a valance, consider how the fabric would look on all of the elements, not just the curtains.

CASE STUDY (OPPOSITE):

The objective in this dining room was to soften the room (which previously had no window treatment), without blocking the view. Sheer, unlined curtains on thin bronze poles with rings were the solution. Instead of trim we added a 2 ½-inch contrast cuff in the same material but a different color on the leading and bottom edges. The adjacent living room curtain fabric is the same, but with a different contrast color on the cuff. Although you cannot see it here, the similar curtain treatment in the two rooms helps unite them, while the different color fabric on the edge defines the two rooms as separate spaces.

This is a good example of a successful window treatment in a challenging architectural environment. Not only were we concerned with preserving the view and the light at all costs, but we had to deal with the fact that the air conditioners run across the bottoms of the windows, preventing the curtains from reaching the floor, as they typically do. Because the curtains are light and airy and similar in tone to the wall color, they do not appear to stop abruptly at the air-conditioning units. Instead, they seem to float above them without drawing attention to their shortened length.

Chapter 8: Adding Color

IN THIS CHAPTER, WE FOCUS ON HOW TO CHOOSE PAINT COLORS AND PAINT FINISHES. WE ALSO LOOK AT WALL-PAPER AND WALL UPHOLSTERY, TWO OTHER EFFECTIVE METHODS OF BRINGING COLOR, PATTERN, AND TEXTURE TO THE WALLS. FINALLY, WE LOOK AT HOW COLOR IS ADDED TO WALL PANELING AND WOOD FLOORS.

PAINT IS ALWAYS OUR FAVORITE PART OF ANY PROJECT. THE VARIOUS COLOR AND APPLICATION TECHNIQUES ARE LIKE THREADS THAT WEAVE THROUGH YOUR ROOMS SUP-PORTING THE RHYTHM AND HARMONY ESTABLISHED BY THE HARD AND SOFT MATERIALS. THERE ARE SO MANY PERMUTATIONS OF EVERY PAINT COLOR THAT YOU CAN ALWAYS BUY OR MIX THE PERFECT ONE—AND PAINT IS NEVER OUT OF STOCK AND RELATIVELY EASY TO CHANGE.

OPPOSITE:
Here is the ultimate in paint for an entry foyer, a custom stencil introducing all the colors in the house. The design includes the client's favorite motif—snakes—woven with her initials into a curvilinear design. An overwash of gold highlights the stencil and brings the walls to life.

Walls

CHOOSING COLORS. This is a subjective, even emotional decision, but it does not need to be a difficult one. Take a moment to gather your thoughts on color and reflect on your visual goals. Initially, consider whether you want a monochromatic scheme or one that embraces a broader, more varied palette from room to room. A monochromatic house can be filled with rooms all of one color, shades of one color, different paint techniques using one color, or some combination of the above. The openness of a monochromatic palette can help emphasize a great view or a distinctive art collection. Or it may be an effective way to express your desire for simplicity or tranquility.

Maybe you prefer an assemblage of colors. From the clarity of two colors to the variety in jewel-like tones of red, green, and blue, if a multi-colored house reflects your aesthetic sensibilities, then that is what you should create.

Your ultimate goal is to distribute colors and techniques so that the flow from room to room is neither drearily stagnant nor excessively jarring. Color is really defined by what surrounds it. The same beige will have a yellow, pink, or green cast depending on what is next to it.

REFER TO YOUR PALETTE. The easiest way to select wall color is to refer back to the palette already elected for the rug and fabrics in the room. In a room without a rug, such as a bathroom or a kitchen, color inspiration may come from the hard materials, such as the wood or stone. On the other hand, you need not be limited by what is available or what has been selected already. Feel free to mix colors or to find a color that does not appear yet but may provide the missing link between the other elements.

ABOVE:
In the stencil illustrated on the previous page the initial G was registered in four different directions, adding movement and another design within the design.

RIGHT:
Ellie's New York City living room is painted with Venetian stucco in a warm, rich terra-cotta color that was overwashed in gold for a bit of shimmering glamour that complements her art and antiques.

TRUST YOUR OWN TASTE. Do not ignore your instinctive reactions to colors that resonate for you. Just like people, different colors have different personalities. Color choices may be stimulated by a feeling or memory of a place once visited. Look to the colors of your garden or the sand at the beach. Explore the pages of a magazine or an art book. One word of warning: Try not to confuse the colors you like to wear with the colors for your walls. Your wardrobe palette and your decorating palette are not the same, and the colors of your clothing might not be appropriate colors to live with in your home.

DISREGARD THE RULES. Do not impose outdated or undue restrictions on your color choices. We feel that the only legitimate rule is that location should not limit your color choice. Instead of following the old dictum to avoid dark walls for a small room, use a deep hue to create an intimate space. The right shade is the one that reflects your fabric and rug schemes, and it is the one you like best.

CHANGE COURSE AS NECESSARY. This is an important point to remember: If something does not feel right, do not be afraid to change it.

Choosing Paint Techniques

It is not enough to tell your painter that you want pale blue walls. Different methods of applying paint produce different effects, so familiarize yourself with the benefits of each. You would not want to use the same style of painting in every room or even in adjacent rooms. The different painting techniques should lead to and complement each other.

PLAIN PAINT. We use this all the time, because it is an easy and relatively inexpensive way to get color on the walls. If you are undecided, you can buy a pint and paint it on the walls to see if you like a hue, instead of trying to gauge the full impact from a tiny paint swatch. Those little color chips simply do not give you enough information to make a final decision. You can always mix a color with white to achieve a lighter shade. But be sure to keep track of the exact mix, so that you can order the same color in the future when you touch up or repaint a wall.

DECORATIVE PAINT. As an alternative to plain paint, we recommend the unique and compelling beauty of decorative painting. A professional painter can prep the walls, but decorative painting techniques require the talents of a specially trained artist. To help you decide on the best technique for your interior, look everywhere for possible ideas—in magazines and books, in showcases, and at friends' houses. The main decorative painting techniques are glazing, stucco, distemper, stenciling, hand painting, and murals.

ABOVE:
When glaze is applied with a comb, it looks very open and adds great depth to the walls. Here the paint is applied in two directions, whch creates a ginghamlike texture.

OPPOSITE:
This blue bedroom in South Carolina was finished with Venetian stucco rather than a glaze. Because this room was very large in scale (25 x 26 feet), stucco, with its greater depth than a simple glaze or plain paint, added a weightiness (in the positive sense) appropriate to the architecture.

GLAZES. When pigments are suspended in a translucent medium, the result is a color complexity not found in plain paint. The interplay between the ground and the translucent color (or colors) allows you to create subtle color effects. Not only can you create a final tone that is both blue and yellow, or perhaps celadon with a gold shimmer, but the colors can also appear to change over the surface. The different glazing methods give the wall color more character and depth by allowing the base color to show through. A room with glazed walls feels luminous and alive.

Glaze techniques, such as strié, crosshatch, stippling, and ragging are some of our favorites. A strié is a very thin, variegated stripe, often in one color, although it can be more than one. Strié is also called "dragging," because it is created by dragging the brush through the paint. A crosshatch is created when the strié is applied in two different directions, resulting in a fabriclike quality. Different effects are created by the use of different brushes, combs, and steel wool. A stipple is a tight application of glaze achieved with a coarse, dense brush. Ragging refers to the technique of removing the paint with a rag after application. A good artist can work with the paint to create a wide variety of finishes from a loose, cloudy effect down to a tight, almost matte surface.

Since glazes are usually applied over oil-based paint, they are more durable and easier to clean than plain painted walls. The color and sheen variation in a multicolored glazed wall makes it more forgiving to normal wear and tear than a smoothly painted wall. Acrylic glazes applied to acrylic bases dry quickly, which means you will have limited time to change the color before you are done. Books on decorative paint will give you detailed technical information, and you should familiarize yourself with the different applications to broaden your choices.

FAUX FINISHES. Glazes can be used to mimic wood grain and marble. Beautiful to look at in their own right, faux finishes are also good problem solvers. For example, a metal door—such as a fire door, an entry door, or an elevator door—can be made to resemble the wood doors throughout the rest of the house when painted with faux wood grain. Faux finishes are also an elegant way to emphasize tradition and to add color. Usually, we do not recommend painting something faux wood or marble that would not normally be made of wood or stone. Also, we use faux finishes sparingly— because sometimes too much really is too much.

VENETIAN STUCCO. Naturally warm and glossy, a tinted Venetian stucco finish creates a lot of movement across the surface of a wall. Venetian stucco, the most common tinted plaster finish and the most readily available, is created by applying layers of wet, colored plaster with a metal trowel, which burnishes the plaster and leaves behind a smooth, buttery, reflective finish appropriate for any kind of luxurious room. Venetian stucco is somewhat vulnerable, however. The surface can be stained by greasy fingers, so we often wax it to add durability.

INTEGRAL PLASTER OR DISTEMPER. Integral plaster refers to a textured, painted finish that can be applied with a brush, rather than a trowel. Distemper refers to a protein that is added to paint and is characteristic of a group of heavy-bodied paints. Milk paint is a type of distemper paint. There are many variations of color with both techniques, and you can even layer on multiple colors or wash a metallic color over regular paint colors. Although both techniques add character, an interesting distemper finish gives instant age to newly Sheetrocked walls.

Custom stencils. Creating a custom stencil is exciting. You can change the color, the elements or motifs, and the scale until you have something that is unique to your home. The motifs can incorporate something personal into the design, such as your initials or a favorite animal or flower. As with most truly custom work, stenciling is expensive. For this reason, we tend to use it in a small space, preferably in public areas, such as an entry or a powder room, where it will be seen. With a stencil, we can use more than one color and hint at some of the colors that will appear in adjacent rooms. For example, if you use a stenciled design in an entry, the living room walls could be glazed in one of the stencil colors and the dining room walls could have a chair rail with another one of the stencil colors below it. This practice distributes technique and palette over three major rooms.

Pictorial scenes and murals. Even more precious than stencils are pictorial hand-painted scenes and murals, which have two added benefits. First, enveloping the room in a complete work of art eliminates the need to purchase artwork for the space. Second, a long and narrow space can be made more gracious when its perspective is transformed by an artificial vista painted by hand. We often have these murals painted on canvas, which can be removed from the walls and reinstalled if a client relocates.

Gilding. The application of thin sheets of metal to walls, moldings, or furniture is called gilding. Whether the metal is real or composition leaf, gilding will dress up any surface.

OPPOSITE:
The inspiration for these yellow walls came from Ellie's frequent trips to Florence, where she is a founding member of the Friends of Florence board. This recalls the exterior stucco color of one of the famous shops on the Ponte Vecchio.

LEFT:
Celadon-glazed walls are embellished with early American stencils by Teles and Adams. The curvilinear pattern under the crown molding was replicated from one in historic Deerfield Village; the one above the base molding is their own design.

The varying pressure of the artist's hand adds life and openness to a stencil pattern.

ABOVE MIDDLE:
Metallic paint in this stencil shimmers on the walls of a small elevator landing in New York City. To achieve this effect, the walls were base-coated with metallic copper paint, and then a gold stencil was screened on top. The design refers to a Japanese obi brocade.

ABOVE RIGHT:
Panels of *églomisé*—reverse painting on glass—add detail to the woodwork of this dressing room, which is glazed, stenciled, and gilded.

RIGHT:
A gilded convex mirror reflects a hand-painted mural. Resting on the mantel is a superb pair of lions carved in pine and a pair of Chinese export porcelain dinner plates.

Paint Finishes

The basic types of finishes refer to the amount of sheen in the paint. Flat finishes have very little or no sheen. Enamel paints have an increasing amount of sheen from eggshell to satin to semigloss and gloss. Flat paint does not show imperfections, but it marks easily. As the paints increase in sheen, they show more flaws, but they are more durable. As with every other decorating decision, you need to balance function with design considerations.

When walls are to be plain painted, we recommend flat latex because the imperfections are less visible. When glazed, walls must be prepared with a skim coat, one coat of primer, and two coats of satin Impervo before the glaze.

The Decorator's Painting Tools

PAINT SCHEDULES. Just as we refer to a floor plan in making decisions about furniture selection, we make a paint schedule to serve as a kind of road map for the paint plans. Sometimes it is hard to figure out what colors you want each room to be, or even to remember what colors or techniques are going to be next to each other. With this tool, we can orchestrate the colors and textures in every room and establish overall color schemes by seeing how wall finishes relate in adjacent rooms.

There are two kinds of paint schedules—the artistic and the technical. The artistic schedule is a simple, graphic way to figure out your preferred overall background color minus any decorative techniques. Color in the edges of the rooms on the floor plan with a colored pencil or a mix of

LEFT:
This graceful stencil is quite complex. A damask pattern was applied on a beige-glazed ground. The intricate line work was then outlined in gold paint, leaving the impression of an embroidered fabric on the walls.

pencils that approximate the dominant color of the walls. Another helpful visual tool is to insert a swatch of fabric for the furniture upholstery into the floor plan as a reference to the background color of the fabrics. With these methods, it is easy to study the relationships between rooms. You will quickly see if you have two green rooms in a row or if they are clashing in some way. All the rooms should flow together without repetition—unless, of course, monochrome is your theme.

The technical schedule is a chart that includes all specifications (paint, wallpaper, upholstered walls, paneling) for all surfaces, including walls, ceilings, and woodwork. Set up this schedule early in the construction project for budget estimating, because this is the one that describes how to prep the walls and other surfaces.

COLOR SAMPLE BOARDS. When working with glazes or other decorative techniques, ask the artist to make sample boards of possible choices to help finalize combinations of colors and finishes. A sample board is a piece of Masonite or some other thin but sturdy material upon which the painter can try out various colors and techniques. A color sample board should measure about 12 by 15 inches so that it is not too cumbersome to carry around. The boards should be prepped to the same specifications as the walls, i.e., with the same base coat. This will insure that the finishes will appear on the walls exactly as they do on the sample boards.

We play with a shade by adding various tints, which we refer to as hues, and by tweaking it lighter or darker, changing its value until we get it right. Sometimes we ask the painter to make multiple samples of one technique, making the paint more or less active and more or less translucent. It takes time to work out the optimum wall color and treatment. But working on boards is like research and shortcuts the process in the end. Once a sample is approved, meet your painter at the site to try it in a small area before the entire room is painted, because the paint can look different on site. The color may need just a bit more adjusting before it is ready to go on the walls.

Wallpaper

Do not overlook wallpaper as an effective way to bring color and pattern to your walls. It is good to have another wall treatment besides paint in the overall mix of your house, but like anything else, do not use it everywhere. Papers without patterns, such as grass cloth and bark paper, add texture and work well in any room, from a gym to a library, dining room, or bedroom. Wallpaper is also great in closets, where it acts like a contrasting lining in an overcoat or a suit jacket.

Of course, wallpaper is not just for closets and backgrounds. Wallpapers were the first hand-blocked stencils and were also often hand-painted. Many of today's papers are adapted from historical designs, and there are some extraordinary antique papers available. These can be very inspiring and can make an impressive statement if you choose to use them.

We do not use wallpaper in bathrooms and kitchens, because it is not practical. Wallpaper will peel and mold with humidity, and it stains easily. Another caveat is that some wallpapers, like some tiles, tend to enjoy short periods of popularity in the marketplace and can quickly become unfashionable.

To choose wallpaper, do not look at it on a tabletop. Instead, tape it up on the wall before making a final decision. Always look at samples on a surface that is similar to the surface where they will ultimately be seen. A lamp should be looked at on a table, a carpet on the floor, and wallpaper on the wall.

Look at wallpaper designs the way you look at fabric designs. They have color and scale, and they can be curvilinear or relatively geometric. In Chapter 5, we recommended that you mix patterns as though you were getting dressed, paying particular attention to scale. Now it is time to extend that principle to your walls. For example, if the primary fabric in your room—perhaps the curtain fabric—is a multicolor check, select a wallpaper pattern in a curvilinear floral on a larger scale, or select a textured wallpaper. Add some solid textured fabric on the upholstery to bring out your favorite colors in the pattern, and perhaps find a carpet with a small geometric design to anchor the room. Design the pillows with different patterns and colors as accents.

The key to mixing patterns in a room is to change the scale of the patterns from one material to the next. This holds true for a monochromatic room or a multicolored room. Confirm that there is always a solid expanse somewhere in the room to rest your eyes. This could be the ceiling, the carpet, or the painted walls.

PRACTICAL CONSIDERATIONS. Ordering wallpaper is like order-ing fabric. It comes in a precut roll with a width and a length and a repeat. As with fabric, do not estimate the amount you need yourself. Let the professionals help you. The wallpaper hanger should come to the space or review the elevations and take measurements based on the dimensions of the actual paper you have chosen. Order what he tells you he needs, because only he will know for sure how much waste there will be and how the pattern will lay out.

If you decide to use wallpaper, be aware that European and American rolls come in different sizes. Before you place your order, make sure you get a sample from the current stock available in the warehouse because, like fabric, wallpapers come in dye lots, which may have slight color vari-ations from time to time.

Wall Upholstery

A more opulent alternative for walls is fabric. This can be done in one of two ways. Either the fabric is stretched on panels that are then attached to the walls. Or the fabric is applied to the walls over a thin, acrylic bat-ting material (usually about ¼ inch thick). Do not be afraid to use silks, linen, wool or cotton, any of which could be smooth or woven, hand painted, or embossed. Like wallpaper, fabric on the walls adds a design

element that needs to be evaluated for its color (monochromatic or mul-ticolored, tonal or solid), its pattern (curvilinear or geometric or solid), and its scale (large or small).

Finished upholstered walls are soft and shaded and slightly springy to the touch. In a den or family room with an elaborate audio-visual system, the added wall fabric augments acoustics and feels cozy and quiet—perfect for curling up with a good movie. Luxurious upholstered walls are also one of our favorite treatments for dining rooms and master bedrooms.

PRACTICAL CONSIDERATIONS. For wall upholstery, cover the staples all along the edges, including around the doors and windows and along the molding, with a decorative self welt or a flat tape. For extra articulation, we sometimes add nail heads over the tape. Remember that

OPPOSITE:
Handmade Vietnamese bark paper adds an understated matte texture to the walls. (Stephen Miller Siegel, architect)

ABOVE:
To unify the four different elevations of this study, the same embroidered silk from India was used for both the curtains and the wall upholstery.

upholstered walls are thicker than painted or paper ones, but they should not project past the baseboard or the chair rail. Be sure to tell your contractor as soon as possible which walls are to be covered with fabric so that he can accommodate this. Sometimes the fabric has to be backed with another material before it can be used on the walls. Often the fabric label actually specifies the need for a knit backing to be used for seating and wall upholstery. But if you are unsure, give the upholsterer a sample of the fabric, and he will tell you if it needs a knit or other kind of backing applied.

Upholstering the walls can be expensive because of the labor involved and also because you need a lot of fabric to cover your walls—in fact, much more than you need for your sofa! We like to upholster walls if there is a chair rail in the room. We then need less fabric than if we went from floor to ceiling. And the fabric, which can be delicate, will be better protected from wear and tear. So upholster your walls sparingly, and choose the rooms that you upholster with caution.

For a similar look that is far less expensive, fabric can be acrylic-backed and applied with either glue or adhesive strips (like wallpaper). The appearance is flatter and less formal. If the fabric is applied carefully, you will not necessarily need a trim around all of the edges where the fabric butts up to the moldings.

Wall Preparation

Before a drop of paint touches a brush or the wallpaper is unrolled, the walls need to be prepared and primed correctly. Preparation is essential for long-term beauty and successful results. How much time you spend on prep is the difference between a good job and a bad one. With good prep, your walls will be ready for any kind of decorative treatment you choose.

Tell your painter that good preparation is important to you, and ask what kind of prep he recommends based on the final plan for your paint. The basic process includes filling any inconsistencies in the walls, and then sanding them so they are smooth enough for the layers of paint to adhere properly or for the wallpaper to go on evenly. Cullman & Kravis prep standards always include a skim coat of plaster for a perfectly smooth and fresh base surface, although this adds to the cost. A good primer and a sealer must be used to avoid flashing, which occurs when the paint absorbs differently in different spots, creating a variation in the sheen across the wall's surface. The layers of primer and paint must all be compatible. Flashing may not be apparent right away, but it will become so later on, much to your regret. Furthermore, without the right preparation, if a layer of paint is applied directly over an older layer, the new paint will peel because the layers will not adhere.

RIGHT:
Sage-green Ultrasuede, backed with acrylic and hung like wallpaper, covers the walls in a gentleman's library and acts as a softly textured foil for the anigre cabinetry. The underside of the beam around the ceiling and the door to the bathroom were faux-painted to match the stained wood of the room.

Your painter's costs should include all of the prepping and priming required for an adequate paint job. Remember that you get what you pay for—good prep costs money, but is well worth it. You will find that much of the difference in a painter's price will be directly tied to the costs associated with the preparation of the walls, so it may be wise in the long run to spend more if you can afford it. With construction, the contractor often finishes the walls through the prep stage and should give you a price for doing so.

Wood Trim

Painted wood trim is an important partner to the physical walls. When we speak of trim, we are including all window frames, moldings, built-in bookcases, and shelves. Although painted in conjunction with the walls, trims should be painted in a different color and finish to distinguish between wall and woodwork. We often paint the woodwork white to emphasize the definition between the wall and the ceiling or the wall and the door. If not white, they may be glazed in a color that complements the walls or faux-painted a wood color. When trim is plain painted in a color, it tends to look plastic. Plaster molding should be painted in an eggshell finish, and wood moldings in a satin Impervo.

Ceilings

We have already discussed the architectural merits of ceilings in Chapter 3, but you should also consider the decorative merits of painting or papering a ceiling. The hint of color in a glazed ceiling softens the contrast between the wood walls and the ceiling of a paneled room. A lightly tinted ceiling imparts a feeling of age to an antique paneled room. You might glaze or stencil the flat panels of a coffered ceiling to add definition. If you like a reflective finish on ceilings, as we do, why not apply gold leaf to the ceiling of a powder room, or stencil the ceiling of a dressing room to create your own little jewel box of a space? Ceilings are generally painted in flat latex (again because of the issue of masking imperfections). When glazed, the ceilings must be finished like the walls with satin Impervo.

You could also employ gold or silver tea paper in the panels. Tea paper is a very thin and flexible paper, traditionally made with gold or silver leaf, although today it is usually made with metals resembling gold and silver. Tea paper is available in smaller dimensions than a roll of wallpaper (usually in pieces measuring 16 by 22 inches). The smaller pieces can be placed inside a shaped ceiling coffer much more easily than a stiff paper.

"Even if you have a monochromatic palette, it is a good idea to change the painting technique from one room to the next to avoid repetition."

Left:
All of the woodwork in this dressing room is glazed, stenciled, and edged with gold. The barrel-vaulted ceiling is gilded with aluminum leaf and over-glazed with a golden wash of color.

FLOORS

Staining

Although it is possible to stain your floors on your own, this is a job best done by a professional for optimal results. We can approximate the desired color by trying different stains on small samples. However, we never make a final decision until we have mixed the colors on site, together with the contractor who will be finishing the floor, to see the color on the actual wood in the true light of the room. On an out-of-town project a few years ago, it seemed extravagant to fly across the country just to mix the floor color. We asked the contractor to send us a sample floorboard stained with a particular color mix. Once we approved the sample in New York, we told him to go ahead with the floors. On our next site visit, to our surprise, we saw a bright pumpkin-color floor! The light in a faraway job site can be different from the light in Manhattan, and our stain mix, which was perfect for oak flooring on the East Coast, was all wrong for oak flooring on the West Coast.

RIGHT:
The graceful ellipse of the staircase that John B. Murray designed for this Manhattan duplex frames the view of the entry floor, which is hand-painted and stenciled in a Regency motif.

OPPOSITE:
The floors of this beach house were all stained dark to ground the house and lend an air of solidarity and age to the vaulted spaces. The dark stain is repeated in the stair cap and the dark tones of the furniture.

Our usual way to stain and finish a floor is as follows: First, the floor must be sanded. An optional second step is to use water to "pop" the grain and help the stain absorb. (But the deeper color bite can make the floor look more dramatic or even zebra striped.) Then the floor is stained, usually with a combination of favorite colors, such as special walnut, dark walnut, golden oak, natural, and cherry, until the color is appropriate for the design of the particular residence.

Stenciling

Stenciling a wood floor with paint allows you to add decorative color to your flooring in a less formal way than with a marble floor and in a more original way than with standard tile. Stenciling also adds pattern and color without a need to re-lay the boards or add a carpet. A stenciled floor will require some prep work. But your painter will advise you on the best method, which usually involves applying paint on top of raw floorboards and sealing it afterward. Painting a floor can be a costly endeavor, more suitable for small spaces such as entries or powder rooms.

Sealing

The next step after applying the stain is to apply a coat of sealer. There are many finish variations for sealing after the stain is applied, but as a general rule, whatever material you seal with—oil or water— should be the same as the material you finish with. Remember that you have to wait one or two days between coats, so all of this takes a long time to complete. The floor is "screened" between coats to remove any raised areas of debris, dust, or brush bristles, and to leave a super-smooth finish. The final coat of water or oil-based polyurethane is now ready to go on.

We specify either a water- or oil-based polyurethane finish or a waxed finish. Wax has an appealing, subtle sheen and ages well with a lovely patina. But a waxed floor needs buffing every month. An oil-based polyurethane finish has a highly desirable lustrous sheen and is easy to manipulate in the application, because it dries more slowly than a water-based finish. Water-based sealers are not scratch-resistant (the floor will literally scratch if something sharp touches it), but are very durable overall. Even though you must refinish the entire floor for any repairs, most people choose a strong water-based poly for their floors. When you use oil-based poly, the floor takes a long time to finish—often up to two weeks of drying because of the time needed between coats. We recommend an oil-based poly finish in kitchens and other wet areas for durability and water resistance. But a wax finish is generally more appropriate in more formal areas, because it is softer looking, though not as long lasting. As an alternative to increase durability, our experts "break the rules" and apply a coat of oil-based polyurethane, followed by two coats of water-based sealer. With this combination, high traffic areas wear better than with a strictly oil-based finish.

CABINETRY AND PANELING

Ask for paneled rooms and cabinetry to be delivered in a raw state, not pre-finished. Pre-finished wood has a commercial-looking lacquer finish that cannot be adjusted on site, or even touched up when it wears. Also, it is very difficult to change the finish without changing the cabinets.

Wood comes in a variety of species and can be stained in a wide array of colors. There is a lot of artistry involved in staining. Wood has so much pattern and directional variation within each board and from one

This library is in a large beach house with wide expanses of windows and gracious wrap-around porches that capture the views and the sunlight. We were faced with the dilemma of how to finish the library—the only room with just one small window. Rather than use light-color finishes, we emphasized the intimate feeling of the room with a dark French-polished finish on the mahogany cabinetry. The owner says that this is the space where he likes to "hunker down" with his cognac when the storms come.

The C&K Way: Protecting Wood Floors

ONE OF THE DRAWBACKS TO BEAUTIFULLY FINISHED WOOD FLOORS IS THEIR PROPENSITY FOR SCRATCHES, PARTICULARLY IN HIGH-TRAFFIC AREAS, SUCH AS THE KITCHEN AND ENTRY. WE POLITELY REFER TO MINOR MARKS AND SURFACE IMPERFECTIONS AS "CHARACTER." ALTHOUGH NO ONE CAN GUARANTEE A COMPLETELY SCRATCH-FREE SURFACE, YOU CAN TAKE SOME PRECAUTIONS TO REDUCE THE POSSIBILITY. HERE ARE A FEW EASY THINGS ANYONE CAN DO TO MAINTAIN A FLOOR'S FINISH:

*BE SURE TO COVER THE FEET OF CHAIRS AND TABLE LEGS WITH FELT PADS (AVAILABLE AT MOST ANY HOME OR HARDWARE STORE).

*REMIND YOURSELF AND YOUR GUESTS TO REMOVE HEAVY BLACK-SOLED SHOES AND BOOTS AT THE FRONT DOOR.

*DISCOURAGE YOUR CHILDREN FROM RIDING BIKES OR OTHER TOYS INDOORS, AND REFRAIN FROM USING A STROLLER IN THE HOUSE.

*AVOID WEARING HIGH HEELS ON PINE, CHESTNUT, AND OTHER SOFT WOODS.

*RAISE PLANT POTS OFF THE FLOOR WITH A FOOTED PLATE OR TRIVET.

*ASK YOUR FLOOR FINISHER FOR FURTHER MAINTENANCE RECOMMENDATIONS.

board to another that it is important to work with a master craftsman who can blend colors during the staining process. Yet even with an expert cabinetmaker, you should be in control of the color every step of the way to get the shade you desire. After sealing, go look at the color. The more finish steps that have gone by, the harder it is to change the color, because every layer is translucent. As Steve Williams, our favorite wood finisher says, working with wood is not the same as painting, because you are bringing out its beauty instead of covering it. Whatever finish you choose, the process begins with the three S's—sand, stain, and seal—and then the wood needs to be finished somehow, with wax or oil or shellac. It is those final finishes that give the wood—and the room it is in—its greatest character and definition.

Finishes

We treat stained-wood cabinets and paneling like fine furniture. There are a number of finishing options.

Wax. For a natural look and a soft subtle finish, we use clear or tinted wax—a traditional finish that is particularly appropriate for pine and sometimes for oak. Wax helps to rejuvenate wood and gives it a glowing richness. A coat of wax sealer should be applied after the final coat of stain and before the six to eight additional coats of wax. In a kitchen, bath, or bar, where there is water, we prefer an oil-based polyurethane finish rather than wax.

Tung oil. This quick-drying finish is made from pressed seeds that come from the nut of the tung tree. It provides a tough, water-resistant finish that does not darken noticeably with age. Tung oil also imparts a natural-looking, transparent sheen, a little shinier than a wax finish. It is easy to apply and to maintain, as well as being less costly.

French polishing. This is not a product but a system of applying shellac to create an especially elegant finish often found on antiques such as eighteenth-century furniture. Dressy mahogany doors and formal walnut furniture are typically finished with a French polish. There are varying degrees to this finish, from open pore to full French polish. In open pore, you see some texture and a bit less sheen, and we find it a bit less dressy than the sheen of a full French polish. In both instances,

ABOVE:
A translucent wash of white paint on paneled walls softly contrasts with the opacity of the white paint on the wood trim.

OPPOSITE:
Reclaimed birch-board ceiling beams and whitewashed boarding organize the view from this sunroom out into the gardens. The tone of the wood was carefully coordinated with the colors of the floor and the wicker furniture, leaving the natural greens of the plantings inside and out as the design elements.

The C&K Way: No-Fail Paint Guidelines

GENERALLY SPEAKING, OIL-BASED PAINTS GO ON MORE SMOOTHLY THAN ACRYLIC, THEY ADHERE BETTER, AND THE COLORS ARE RICHER. THEY ARE ALSO GOOD MOISTURE BARRIERS, WHICH WILL ALLOW THE FINAL COAT TO LAST, PARTICULARLY UNDER WET CONDITIONS. HOWEVER, THEY TAKE LONGER TO DRY AND THE FUMES CAN BOTHER SOME PEOPLE. MOST OF OUR GLAZES ARE OIL-BASED AS WELL, ALTHOUGH SOME ARE ACRYLIC- OR WATER-BASED. WITH THE LATTER, THE BASE COATS ALSO NEED TO BE WATER-BASED FOR ADHESION. THE PROBLEM WITH ACRYLICS IS THAT BECAUSE THEY DRY QUICKLY AND THE COLORS ARE FLATTER, THERE IS NOT AS MUCH TIME TO PLAY WITH COLOR EFFECTS USING A QUICK-DRYING GLAZE. HOWEVER, SOME ARTISTS WANT TO WORK ONLY WITH ACRYLIC PAINTS BECAUSE OF CONCERNS REGARDING THEIR HEALTH. IN FACT, SOME STATES HAVE RESTRICTED THE USE OF OIL-BASED PAINTS. MANY PAINTERS PREFER LATEX MERELY BECAUSE IT DRIES QUICKLY SO THAT THEY CAN FINISH THE JOB QUICKLY AND CHARGE YOU LESS. BUT YOU MAY ALSO SEE MORE BRUSHSTROKES AND ROLLER MARKS, UNLESS IT IS EXPERTLY APPLIED OVER A WELL-PREPARED SURFACE.

WE RECOMMEND THE USE OF OIL-BASED PRIMER SEALER AND OIL-BASED ENAMEL UNDERBODY UNDER ALL ENAMEL EGGSHELL OR SATIN FINISHES. FINISH COATS SHOULD BE OIL-BASED ENAMEL IN A SATIN OR EGGSHELL FINISH. DON'T FORGET, HOWEVER, THAT IF YOU WANT A HIGH SHEEN IN THE FINAL COAT, YOUR WALLS MUST BE WELL PREPARED BECAUSE THE SHINY FINISH WILL HIGHLIGHT ALL SURFACE IMPERFECTIONS. FLAT FINISHES, WHETHER LATEX- OR OIL-BASED, SHOULD BE APPLIED OVER AN OIL-BASED PRIMER.

REMEMBER THAT YOU CAN SEE THROUGH A GLAZE, SOMETIMES DOWN TO THE BASE COAT, AND THIS IS WHAT MAKES THE FINAL COLORS SO INTERESTING. WHEN YOU ARE GLAZING, THE DECORATIVE PAINTER WILL CONFIRM EVERY BASE COAT COLOR, BECAUSE DIFFERENT FINAL EFFECTS REQUIRE DIFFERENT BASE COATS, AND ONLY THE DECORATIVE PAINTER KNOWS WHAT COMBINATION OF COLORS WAS USED TO GET THE SAMPLE YOU APPROVED.

after the sanding, staining, and sealing, there are many applications of fine layers of shellac that bond and form one thicker layer. Because each new application softens and bonds with the layers below, we consider this an easy-to-maintain, reversible finish. If there is too much sheen, pumice powder and an oil mixture applied to the surface and brushed with the grain will result in a rich satin finish.

Liming or cerusing. In this method, one of the best for oak, the grain is wire-brushed to open the pores. Sometimes the wood is bleached to adjust, lighten, and even remove the color, after which a wax finish is applied. Cerused wood is not very durable.

Pickling. In this method, the wood is sanded and then covered with an oil- or latex-based paint that is thinned out and applied like a stain. After sealing, the surface has an overall white cast, like whitewash. This achieves a relatively casual look that we love to use on a simple wood grain such as pine. It is particularly warm and welcoming in a sunroom or in a country kitchen.

CASE STUDY (OPPOSITE):

This client liked baby blue, which inspired us to lacquer the walls of her Fifth Avenue apartment in her favorite color. Lacquering is a time-consuming process in which a uniform glossy surface is created by applying as many as fifteen coats of paint. The woodwork was dragged with toasty beige paint to make it look less new. Then we filled the room with an eclectic mix of antiques, fine art, finishes, and materials, including the diamond-patterned Sisal carpet. Like a white T-shirt, sisal looks great and works almost everywhere in the city or the country, dressy or informal. Sisal has so many applications that we call it the "universal donor." The minimalist painting is by Blinky Palermo.

RIGHT:
The pine walls were washed with a transparent red glaze, which allows the grain and the knots of the wood to show.

Chapter 9: The Kitchen

A KITCHEN MIGHT INVOLVE A MINIMUM OF DECORATING, BUT IT REQUIRES A LOT OF DECISIONS ABOUT TECHNICAL AND HARD-SURFACE MATERIALS. RENOVATING THIS ROOM IS A MORE SERIOUS MATTER THAN JUST CHANGING THE PAINT OR REUPHOLSTERING THE FURNITURE. WE HAVE TO BEGIN WITH A CLEAR VISION OF WHAT A KITCHEN SHOULD BE. SOME OF US DREAM OF A WORKROOM-ENTERTAINMENT SPACE DESIGNED FOR HANDS-ON COOKING WHENEVER A CROWD CONVENES. OTHERS WANT A GLAMOROUS SHOWPLACE FILLED WITH PROFESSIONAL-QUALITY APPLIANCES. FOR MANY FAMILIES, THE KITCHEN NEEDS TO BE A "MISSION-CONTROL ROOM"—A CASUAL DINING SPACE, HOMEWORK HEAD-QUARTERS, AND MEAL-PREPARATION AREA ALL ROLLED INTO ONE. AND FOR THOSE WHO DO NOT COOK, THE KITCHEN MAY JUST BE A PLACE TO CHILL CHAMPAGNE AND MAKE ESPRESSO. BUT WHAT-EVER YOUR PERSONAL KITCHEN FANTASIES AND FUNCTIONAL REQUIREMENTS ARE, WE BELIEVE THE KITCHEN DESIGN SHOULD FIT IN SEAMLESSLY WITH THE STYLE OF THE REST OF YOUR HOME.

OPPOSITE:
The following three pictures are of a kitchen and breakfast room in Manhattan that was created by gutting three rooms—the original family room, the study, and the dining room—and actually blocking a window for the range. City kitchens are mudrooms, dining rooms, homework stations, play-date central, doghouse, and catering center all rolled into one. (John B. Murray, architect)

Right top:
There is no extraneous information in this city kitchen. Clean, white custom-detailed cabinets with durable granite are set off by reclaimed antique floorboards. French bistro chairs pulled up to the island are made of plastic resin and can be wiped with a damp rag to keep them clean.

Right bottom:
In the connecting breakfast and family room, the same resin design seen on the counter stools is used for the bistro chairs. The sofa is covered in a floral pattern on a coffee-color ground—very forgiving for stains! In the foreground of the photograph, we grouped four small coffee tables instead of one. These tables can be separated and used by the family when eating in front of the television.

Opposite:
This kitchen boasts a stenciled floor painted in a two-tone checkerboard of 16-inch cherry-color squares and a study niche for afternoon homework sessions that require supervision. To make the room feel especially welcoming and less like a workspace, we added bookcases and filled them with family photographs, collections of apothecary jars, and other accessories.

FUNCTION FIRST

From a functional point of view, space planning issues, such as storage and eating areas, should top any list. Whether you are working with a kitchen company, an architect, a decorator, or are creating a kitchen on your own, the following topics will help you identify and narrow your priorities.

STORAGE. A kitchen simply cannot function well unless it is organized and offers sensible storage. Do you prefer open storage—such as glass-front cabinets, open shelves, and overhead pot racks—or closed storage, such as traditional cabinets? Would you consider a mix of the two? Would you like custom storage drawers, such as a drawer with knife cutouts, a pop-up drawer for a mixer, a spice drawer, or custom-fitted drawers for a food processor and its various attachments? Would you like antitarnish felt and felt covers in your silver drawers? What about your serving utensils and platters? Do you have several sets of dishes or glassware that you need to access regularly? What are your pantry needs? Do you require special storage for a wine collection?

ROOM FOR DINING. Most people do not eat every meal in their formal dining room. Unless you have a separate secondary dining area, you will need to devote some kitchen space to casual meals. Which meals are eaten in the kitchen and how often? Do you have room for a breakfast nook with a banquette or a separate table with chairs, or do you prefer a counter with bar stools?

COMMAND CENTRAL. Does your kitchen need to accomplish more than cooking and dining? Is it a de-facto office space? Do you need a desk for a computer and Internet access and multiple phone lines? How about a television and a small sofa? Do you need access to adjacent rooms, such as the mudroom or the laundry room?

ENTERTAINING EXTRAS. If you entertain frequently and require assistance from caterers, you may have some unique concerns. Do you need extra workspace for caterers to prep? Do you need extra storage for party glassware and china? A separate butler's pantry is a useful storage space for liquor and wine, and the extra shelving and cabinets could hold party crystal and glassware.

COOKING CONCERNS. The following questions are best answered by the person in your family who does most of the cooking. First are general appliances: What type of sink, oven, dishwasher, and refrigerator do you prefer? Do you need more than one of these items? What other types of tools and appliances are required? If you have the space or the expertise, what about something extravagant like a wood-burning stove or a rotisserie or a pizza oven? Is there food you prepare that would benefit from a special work area, such as a stepped-down counter for rolling pastry? Does it matter if the dishwasher loads on the right-hand or left-hand side of the sink?

THE WORK TRIANGLE AND BEYOND

The cornerstone of any good kitchen plan is the work-triangle relationship formed by the cooktop, the refrigerator, and the sink. This triangle of necessities should be designed for ease of movement and logical flow. After you have completed the functional analysis for your kitchen, you should determine the placement of the triangle on your floor plan. Consider the mix of volumes, because certain pieces—a double-wall oven or a refrigerator/freezer combination—are bulky. These should be placed in the least conspicuous position to maximize low counter space and to maintain an airy feeling in the kitchen. Even if the position of these three elements does not form a perfect triangle, the kitchen will be better for having them dispersed throughout the volume of the space.

Bigger is not always better. A huge side-by-side refrigerator and freezer is not an elegant solution to your kitchen planning. An oversize refrigerator can be intimidating, and it decreases the amount of usable counter space. And how often do you access a massive freezer? It may be better placed outside the kitchen or in the pantry, if you have one. Consider purchasing small refrigerator drawers for beverages and small freezer drawers for storage or ice and installing them in the lower cabinets.

Be sure to research plenty of technical information about what constitutes a successful working kitchen in the multitude of kitchen-design books and magazines that are readily available.

INGREDIENTS OF A KITCHEN

There is no shortage of visual inspiration when it comes to kitchens. You may admire a friend's colorful country kitchen or find yourself tearing out glossy magazine photos of gleaming stainless-steel workspaces. In a kitchen, response to material and form is often intuitive—you know what you like when you see it. You already considered elements such as woodwork, countertops, and floors when you were choosing your hard materials. But we present here some additional specifics.

Cabinetry

Kitchen cabinetry should relate to the woodwork in the rest of the home. Often the same woodworkers we have worked with elsewhere in a house will build the cabinets and custom-finish the cabinetry on site.

Depending on what may have been unearthed during demolition—chunky gas meters and pipes that cannot be moved—you may find that you have a variety of depths available for base and upper cabinetry, instead of one long, uninterrupted wall. Once the demolition is complete, the cabinetmakers must come to the site to take precise measurements, so that when they build they can allow for all of these variations in the space. From a budget perspective, use standard-size cabinets. Otherwise, a millwork shop will customize cabinets, which are more expensive than standard-size cabinets but maximize use of the available space.

Cabinets come in (or can be designed in) a wide variety of styles. Look at different kitchens before you decide on whether you want overlapped or inset doors, and make notes of hardware options and placement that appeal to you. There are basically two types of cabinet doors: An overlapped door literally overlaps the framework of the cabinetry; an inset door fits into the opening of the cabinet. We prefer the clean elegance of inset doors, because they function better over time and they showcase the skill of the cabinetmaker. An overlapped door, with its concealed hinges, can hide myriad sins, but the hinges often loosen more quickly. We prefer to see an inset door perfectly lined up with its neat attachment of exposed hinges.

While you are working out your cabinetry, also think about where in the kitchen you might like to have bookcases or shelves. Handy for storing cookbooks, shelves add a decorative element, providing an opportunity to display collections, particularly pottery or platters.

Countertops

Keep in mind that the countertop is a very large visual part of your kitchen, so it should be attractive. It is also something that must withstand the rigors of day-to-day use—clanging pots, hot pans, chopping knives, clattering dishes. To this end, we choose materials that are both attractive and easy to clean. We have discussed the use of stone countertops in Chapter 3. We often recommend granite and marble for countertop use, not only because of their fresh look, but also because they can handle hot dishes right off the stove or out of the oven.

OPPOSITE TOP:
In vacation homes such as this Vail penthouse, kitchens are often open to the dining and living spaces. Here family and friends can perch on stools at the kitchen counter or sit at the dining table. Notice the continuity of materials from living spaces to the kitchen. (Gordon Pierce, architect)

OPPOSITE BOTTOM:
Holophane lights punctuate the ceiling of this Manhattan kitchen. The cherry cabinetry is offset with Saint Cecelia stone, a favorite granite because of its cream, beige, and gray palette. (John B. Murray, architect)

ABOVE:
The Costa Esmeralda granite top of the counter is repeated on the backsplash to create a calm kitchen. (John B. Murray, architect)

Although we sometimes use tile or glass for the backsplash, we often recommend keeping the backsplash the same material as the countertop to maintain a consistent horizon line in the kitchen and to limit the variety of materials. And at times, we prefer the combination of neat ceramic tile with a counter of granite or some other stone. A mosaic of stone tiles in different shapes, types, and colors can enhance or contrast with the color of a stone countertop. But try to keep the materials simple. A kitchen is a very expensive room to redecorate, and although pretty tiles are seductive, they can give away the vintage of your kitchen!

When selecting a stone slab for a countertop, the installer cannot depend simply on plan drawings. He must confirm the size and amount of stone slab based on actual on-site measurements made after the cabinets are installed, or at the very least, on an accurate template. You should confirm that the slab will be big enough to create the size counter that you want, or else you should discuss where any seams will be placed.

There is another variable to consider—the edge detail. We generally use stone that is about an inch thick with some sort of shaped edge. We select the details for the edges as carefully as we select the actual stones, because edge designs can affect the look or style of the room. For a country kitchen, we prefer a straight, eased edge. In an urban setting, a more intricate edge is required, with inside and outside hand-carved corners to achieve the quality we look for. Be sure you get an actual sample of the edge before committing to it.

Many people like wood countertops, but wood is soft and easily marred by heat and sharp edges. Wooden counters do not stand up to knives unless they have a true butcher-block surface, and even then, the butcher block is meant to show the marks. So use wood on the counters only if you want to see the wear and tear.

Stainless steel can be very sleek, especially if the kitchen has stainless-steel appliances. It will not be marked by hot pots or dishes, but it is

difficult to clean, scratches easily, and can rust if not maintained properly. Stainless steel can lend a relatively clinical appearance to the room, like a doctor's exam room, and metal pots and pans will make a resonant clank. Zinc is another option.

Flooring

Always install the flooring fully under the appliances for several reasons. Moving an appliance for service or cleaning is often impeded if the flooring does not fully extend under the equipment. Additionally, if the appliance is replaced at a later date, there is no guarantee that it will have the same "footprint," leaving mismatched flooring exposed.

Because it is soft and warm underfoot, we usually choose wood for kitchen floors. Tile and linoleum are also popular and are both easy to clean. Linoleum is quite thin and is set with glue. One potential downside with tile and stone is that they need to be set into mud, which raises the level of the floor. The thickness of wood also raises the floor level, but this can be compensated for with a saddle.

OPPOSITE:
This Hamptons kitchen has a countertop of *pietra serena*, a hardy basalt stone. The backsplash is of hand-made subway tiles in a cream color, which contrasts with the crisp white cabinetry. (Andrew Pollock, architect)

ABOVE LEFT:
The adjacent sitting area in the previous kitchen repeats the charcoal gray of the countertop on the fireplace surround. Portraits of the owner's dogs taken by photographer Neil Winokur grace the fireplace wall. (Andrew Pollock, architect)

ABOVE RIGHT:
The curved Windsor backs of a pair of stools soften the lines in this light-filled kitchen. The ceiling is faux-painted in an interlocking circle design that simulates the pressed tin ceilings of the 19th century. A three-stemmed holophane light is suspended over the central island.

Another popular flooring for kitchens is cork. People are afraid of it because they think it is fragile, but cork is water resistant, and moreover it typically has a sealant. Cork works especially well with underfloor heating, and it is resilient and very comfortable underfoot for long periods. It is a "green" material, as it has traditionally been harvested for centuries from living trees that are not injured in the process. Wood, stone, and ceramic tiles are often also considered "green."

Lighting

We discussed kitchen lighting in Chapter 4, but it bears repeating that light types in the kitchen can be the most varied of any room in the house. Think about installing decorative suspended fixtures over an island or a table or both, with task lights under the counters, and general illumination lights (such as recessed or flush-mounted lights or additional suspended fixtures) around the perimeter of the room. If there is a desk, place a decorative lamp on it. If you have a window or an alcove, include sconces on the sides of the cabinetry surrounding the window.

OPPOSITE:
Finding the right lighting for a kitchen is always a creative challenge. Keeping the metal finish the same on all the different fixtures is a great way to unify your choices. Relating the fixtures to a grid that references the different zones of activity will also guarantee a good lighting plan. Suspended lights hover over the pair of islands, flush-mounted fixtures alternate with recessed lights in the coffers, and six-arm chandeliers light the sitting room and the breakfast area beyond. (Mark Finlay, architect)

ABOVE:
Another view of the same kitchen, which is truly the entertaining center of the house. The pair of islands, plenty of seating, a breakfast area, and an enormous deck are all hard for friends and family to resist.

Right top:
In a residence with an Asian theme (note the Tang dynasty Chinese horse on the sideboard and the Ming wine cooler at the window), Japanese black lacquer trays are used as place mats with gold-lacquered fan plates set to receive the first course.

Right bottom:
In a formal Georgian-style residence, we decided to leave the English three-pedestal dining table uncovered, so the beauty of the 19th-century mahogany could be appreciated. The table is set with "hello" plates in an early 19th-century Coalport Rock and Tree Imari design on top of silverplated chargers with gadrooned borders to prevent the wood from being marked. The handmade sterling flatware is "Fiddle Thread and Shell" and the crystal wine and water goblets are from Baccarat in the "Renaissance" pattern. Sheffield sterling candlesticks and an unusual pair of lacquered George III coasters flank the floral centerpiece.

Tableware and Entertaining

As part of our overall decorating approach, we like to assist our clients in choosing their tableware and linens. We also offer solutions for storage and protection of these items.

China and Tableware

We often ask clients to consider purchasing two groups of china—one to complement the design of the kitchen and breakfast room, and a more formal ensemble to complement the dining room. Gone are the days when everyone had one or two sets of matching china. We like the mix-and-match approach described below.

Charger. If you are entertaining guests, do not set the table with the dinner plate, which should be in the kitchen getting hot or in a line waiting for food. Instead, set the table with a charger of metal, china, or glass. For china chargers, we generally choose white with a border or a matching color; these china chargers can also double as buffet plates.

"Hello" plate. This is typically a smaller decorative or antique plate with an all over design that we place on top of the charger. These are fun to collect, and by keeping the design of your dinner plate simple, you can always find other "hello" sets to use in coordination with your other tableware. This plate can double as your dessert plate, or even as a salad plate, if you have a few sets. When planning to serve the meal from the kitchen directly on the dinner plates, you should set the table with just a charger and the hello plate. This way, the table is not just set with chargers (which can make the table look somewhat bare when you walk into the room).

Dinner plate. We prefer a classic white dinner plate with a simple border of a color and silver or gold. First, white provides a neutral background for the presentation of a beautiful meal. Second, plates with designs in the center tend to get marred and scratched by silverware.

Salad plate. Although the salad plate may match the dinner plate, feel free to find other interesting designs that would complement the dinner plate.

LEFT:
The beige-and-gold English drabware harmonizes with the lyrical Matisse stencil on linen from 1946 called *Oceania, The Sky.*

Coffee and tea cups, saucers. You will want to keep these as simple as possible so they can coordinate with any elaborate or colorful "hello" or dessert plates you might find.

Crystal. Every place setting should have the classic arrangement of glasses for red wine, white wine, and water. We sometimes play with colored glasses for water or white wine, but never for red wine, because it is important to see the color of the wine.

Table Linens

In choosing linens, our motto is to be always prepared for casual and formal dining, and also for different-size parties.

Tablecloth. Start with a polyester or preshrunk cotton tablecloth and buy it in two sizes—the size of your table as it is every day and the size it becomes when it is extended to accommodate additional guests. One set of coordinating napkins will work with both tablecloths. Look also for an inexpensive Scotchgarded fabric in a simple pattern, such as a stripe or a fun plaid. These tablecloths work well for a casual brunch, a casual family dinner, or a kids' party, and stains will be minimal. The next tablecloth is one for company, perhaps in hand-cut linen, organdy, or an embroidered cloth. Again, you may wish to purchase these in two sizes to accommodate different size parties. Special cloths like these require a liner.

A good upholsterer or seamstress can also make tablecloths for you. If you find a cotton fabric you love, make sure that it is washable, or ask your seamstress to pre-shrink it. Your upholsterer or seamstress may be able to supply a stock fabric that is already Scotchgarded, or you can

LEFT:
Setting the table is about creating an ambience with a personal mix of objects. The owner's collection of 19th-century blue-and-white ironstone is the perfect accompaniment for the twelve sculptures of the zodiac signs, which were purchased in Hong Kong and were the genesis for the room's decoration. Although they may seem counterintuitive to the intended formality, everyday rattan place mats add an unexpected twist to this setting.

have it treated. If you are not sure whether a fabric will wear well, buy a yard and try it out. It is always fun to have two or three of these cloths on hand for a dinner party or a luncheon. Our rule is that a tablecloth hangs to the floor or 8 to 10 inches below the tabletop, whichever you prefer. (Do not forget to include the depth of the table pad when measuring for the length.) It is helpful to have your seamstress or upholsterer make a template of the dining table to take into account corners that are rounded or squared off, or to get an accurate measurement of an oval table.

Place mats. Although tablecloths are lovely, it would be a shame to cover a beautiful table all the time, so we also suggest buying a few sets of place mats. Place mats come in many different styles and materials, both casual and formal. Linen place mats are pretty but too thin to protect the table, so you will need plastic liners underneath them. Textured mats, such as bamboo and straw, are always great looking and widely available.

We often make custom wooden mats for each place and finish them with a wood stain, paint, or even lacquer in a wide variety of designs. It is great to have more than one set to suit your entertaining needs. We have created place mats using fabrics that coordinate with our interiors. For an easy-to-care-for place mat, have the fabric laminated and then sent to an upholsterer to be cut and hemmed. There are also many laminated place mats available from better linen shops.

A more elegant option is to use silver service plates and water-glass coasters (to protect against sweating) instead of tablecloths or place mats.

Napkins. Large white squares of linen, either 20 or 22 inches square, are the best. They may have a simple hemstitch, or you might like to embellish them with a small design in the corner or even a monogram. For casual meals, buy some inexpensive napkins and have them stenciled with an initial or a whimsical symbol, such as a zodiac sign. For cocktail napkins, use small linen napkins, also with a hemstitch or small edge detail. These too can be decorated for fun with a small stencil design.

Protective Measures

Table pads. A valuable antique dining table—or any dining table—should be protected at meal times. There are quite a few options available, the first and most obvious of which is a table pad. Many people may remember their mother's table pads, which were probably white vinyl on one side and brown felt on the other. There are still companies that will make these for you by coming to your home and measuring for custom-size table pads. Some have a good selection of colors to choose from, and we definitely recommend a brown faux-wood vinyl rather than white (it is more attractive when visible through a cutwork or openwork tablecloth). Or you may choose a color to go with the décor of the dining room. A simpler and more storage-friendly alternative to the pads is to have simple felt cloths made by your upholsterer or by a fine-linen shop. These can be cut from brown felt or another color that will work with the scheme of the room.

Drawer linings. Wherever you decide to keep your silver—probably in a pantry or sideboard drawer—be sure to line the drawers with protective cloth. We give our cabinetmaker the cloth and the exact measurements of the silver pieces. He will then wrap Masonite drawer dividers with the cloth and line the entire drawer.

You can choose from no-tarnish felt or Pacific cloth or Kenized cloth. No-tarnish and Pacific cloth felts are brown because the silver nitrate particles in the fabric tarnish and change color (a light-colored cloth would appear soiled by the tarnishing). The brown fabric may gradually change to a slightly different shade, but do not attempt to wash it because that will ruin the fabric. Pacific cloth is available in 36-inch-wide bolts and is generally regarded as the most effective no-tarnish cloth on the market.

Kenized cloth is very similar, but it is available in other colors you may prefer. The zinc nitrate particles suspended in the fabric do not darken with tarnishing over time, which allows for the wider color range. Kenized cloth is sold by the yard in 57-inch-wide bolts.

Do You Know? Kitchen Elevations

KITCHEN ELEVATIONS SHOULD INCLUDE THE PLACEMENT OF APPLIANCES AND FIXTURES USING THE ACTUAL EXAMPLES YOU HAVE CHOSEN AND THE PLACEMENT OF ALL HARDWARE USING THE ACTUAL HARDWARE. ONCE THE FIXTURES AND HARDWARE ARE CHOSEN, THE SPECS MUST BE SENT DIRECTLY TO THE ARCHITECT OR CONTRACTOR SO THEY CAN BE INCLUDED IN THE DRAWINGS.

CASE STUDY #1:

The challenge in this kitchen was to create something new but to remain consistent with the overall style of the house, a sprawling Tudor revival filled with rich materials and antiques. The client asked that the kitchen plan tie into the flow of the entire house, so all of the principal circulation routes of the house were designed to feed into the kitchen octagon. This unique shape becomes the nucleus of the house. With a commanding octagonal island in its center, the kitchen engages the major corridors and rooms in the house and also connects to the exterior gardens. One side of the island faces the pantry and larder; other sides face the butler's pantry, the main entrance corridor of the house, the service counter and the breakfast room, and even outside in the direction of the potting shed.

Because the view and the light from the small windows on either side of the range were limited in this country kitchen, the architect, Ira Grandberg, added the dramatic skylight above the central island in order to send natural light down into the interior of the kitchen. Glowing with sunlight, the island is visible all day from the various visual axes, and the eye is drawn to the kitchen as the central hub.

Although the kitchen is composed of mostly new materials, we didn't want it to stand out like a shiny new room in a gracious old house. One way to address this was to incorporate an antique element, so the brick backsplash in the cooking area of the kitchen was made from the exterior wall of an old shed. The contrast between new and old materials—the stainless-steel appliances and countertops vs. the texture of the antique brick backsplashes—is one of the highlights of the kitchen. (Ira Grandberg, architect)

ABOVE:
A collection of botanical plates adds color to this monochromatic kitchen.

CASE STUDY # 2:

This kitchen presents a study in contrasts. Our clients wanted a country feeling with elegant city details. The space had to be formal enough for catered parties, but informal enough for a weeknight family dinner and for the kids to hang out after school.

A kitchen has to address as many needs as it can within the limitations of the space available, a situation that is intensified in an urban apartment. Here we set up three basic areas: the main workspace, the breakfast room, and the butler's pantry. To keep things airy in the main two-thirds of the kitchen, we redistributed the refrigeration bulk by placing the freezer in the breakfast room.

The pantry is connected to the entry foyer and thus to guests or to a party, because it really functions as an entertainment space, not as part of the kitchen. To make it more formal than the other areas, we finished the mahogany cabinetry with a glossy French polish.

In the rest of the space, we evoked a country feeling with the hard materials. Bright green *verde esmeralda* marble counters, both durable and refined, suited the needs of our client perfectly. The simple wood floor furthers the country effect. We used a wide plank with a staggered running bond (where the boards connect end to end in a linear pattern but without lining up the seams) and no border. This flooring ties in with those in the rest of the apartment, which are the same species and stain color but with borders. We avoided using the border here because it would have made the kitchen feel smaller than it actually is. The decorative holophane lighting fixtures also helps add to the aesthetic we desired. Their linear sophistication brings a touch of industrial urban chic to the country style of the kitchen design. (Elliot Rosenblum, architect)

ABOVE LEFT:
A mahogany butler's pantry with granite countertops and smoked mirror backsplash.

ABOVE RIGHT:
The backsplash of beige tumbled marble with green accents from the green marble of the countertop.

OPPOSITE:
The breakfast room of our case study. The shirred curtains in the glass-fronted cabinetry provide screening for items stored out of view.

Chapter 10: Bathrooms and Closets

Bathrooms

SQUARE FOOT FOR SQUARE FOOT, YOU PROBABLY GET MORE MILEAGE FROM YOUR BATHROOMS THAN FROM, SAY, YOUR DINING ROOM. WHEN YOU THINK ABOUT IT, THE BATHROOM IS USUALLY WHERE YOU START YOUR DAILY ROUTINE OF SHOWER AND SHAVE OR MAKEUP, AND ALSO WHERE YOU BRING YOUR DAY TO A CLOSE, TOOTHBRUSH IN HAND. FOR THESE REASONS, YOUR BATHROOM SHOULD BE TREATED AS A ROOM LIKE ANY OTHER—WITH JUST AS MUCH CONSIDERATION GIVEN TO SPACE PLANNING, ARCHITECTURAL DETAILS, AND DECORATIVE DESIRES. AND AS WITH OTHER ROOMS, IT IS BEST TO DETER-MINE YOUR BATHROOM PLANS AT THE BEGINNING OF THE RENOVATION OR CONSTRUCTION PROCESS, IN ORDER TO ADDRESS SUCH TASKS AS PLUMBING AND TILING WHILE EVERYTHING ELSE IS ALSO UNDER CONSTRUCTION.

OPPOSITE:
In the master bath, matching his and her vanities divided by a tub are all clad in yellow-tinted satinwood called avodire. An antique alabaster light casts a graceful glow on the vaulted ceiling. (John B. Murray, architect)

The Foolproof Classic Bathroom

Our designs are clean and functional, with effective lighting, hard materials, and hardware that speak the same language and are of the same quality as those in the rest of the house. As with kitchens, we keep the details relatively simple and classic. Regardless of who is going to use the bathroom, you cannot go wrong with fixtures that are mostly white or off-white—sinks, toilets, and baths—and mostly white woodwork and white towels. You can always convey a secondary palette through accent tiles or stones, the glazing or painting of walls and woodwork, the fabrics used for curtains, and embroidery threads on towel designs and other decorative objects.

A classic bathroom will also prove valuable when it comes time for resale. A bathroom can be tailored to reflect your stylistic wishes. But if reselling your home is ever going to be an option, you should keep your bathrooms relatively neutral. Creating a pink-and-white, nursery-themed bathroom for your baby daughter will seem very limiting if prospective buyers have two teenage boys, not to mention how your daughter will feel when she grows up. People do think about these things when they look for a new home.

Required Elements

Your checklist for each bathroom and powder room includes choosing the fixtures within the limits of the space, selecting fittings (sink and shower handles and spouts) and hardware (knobs, pulls, hinges, and towel bars) and lights, dedicating storage space, and choosing your bathroom linens.

FIXTURES AND SPACE ALLOTMENT. What are your essential bathroom elements? Will they fit in the space? Identifying your fixture preferences and their combinations: a toilet, a sink, a pair of his-and-her's sinks, a bathtub, a shower/bath, a separate shower, and so on. If you have the space, a separate WC, with a window if possible, is a truly functional luxury. Sinks are easier on your back at a height of 33 to 34 inches, rather than the U.S. standard sink height of 30 inches.

FITTINGS AND HARDWARE. We prefer polished nickel for the bathroom fittings because it is warmer and less commercial looking than polished chrome. But chrome is bright and fresh, and always affordable and appropriate. Antiqued or burnished brass is also suitable in a powder room or in any bathroom that you feel is more formal than the others. Here are a few general guidelines we follow.

For the fittings, use comfortable and ergonomic levers or cross-handle styles rather than spheres or something else that is hard to grab when your hands are wet. Keep the same finish from sink to shower, and be sure the doorknobs inside the bathroom are in the same finish as the fittings (although they may be different on the opposite side of the door). Even the flush knob on the toilet should match.

The C&K Way: Good Architecture in a Tiny Space

IN CHAPTER 3, WE MADE A CASE FOR THE IMPORTANCE OF ARCHITECTURE IN RELATION TO DECORATING, AND THIS THEORY TRICKLES DOWN TO THE BATHROOMS WE DESIGN. EVEN IN THE TINIEST POWDER ROOMS, ALL WALLS HAVE A BASE MOLDING AND CROWN, OR MAYBE A CHAIR RAIL AND WAINSCOTING. WHEN YOU DEFINE THE WALLS WITH ARCHITECTURAL DETAILS, THE ROOM WILL AUTOMATICALLY LOOK BIGGER, WHICH IS A HELPFUL ILLUSION FOR A BATHROOM.

RIGHT:
To augment the view and balance the existing window, we added a mirror in the same form as the adjacent windows to create a whimsically shaped room. The domed ceiling is faux-painted to look like the sky. The floor is faux-painted as well, with a mariner's compass motif. (Elliot Rosenblum, architect)

OPPOSITE:
His and her vanities are separated by a built-in window seat, which doubles as a hamper. The central slab of Calacatta marble is almost four feet in diameter. In the shower, slabs of Crema Delicato marble are as large as 4 feet by 4 ½ feet. All slabs were selected at a marble yard, and templates were created for each so that the veining would be pleasing. (John B. Murray, architect)

Towel bars. Towels should always be close at hand. Place them on a wall, on or near the sink, shower, and bathtub. Mount a towel bar to the side of the vanity for a convenient hand towel. Hooks are good, too, where space is tight. Try not to wait until you are done with the bathroom to decide where you would like bars and hooks to go. It is better to have your carpenter install blocking because these items need extra support within the wall. Within the shower area, the towel bar will be mounted to the tile. Again, you should have a professional do this properly, so that the tile or marble does not break.

Mirrors. In addition to the vanity or medicine cabinet mirror, give yourself a wall-mounted, small-size mirror with magnification. Some designs are available with a small light inside the mirror, which greatly facilitates shaving and eyebrow plucking! Specify the location for the mirror prior to construction, preferably on the elevation drawing, because these mirrors usually need some sort of extra support in the wall. If it is illuminated, ask your electrician to mount a junction box behind it in order to provide power.

LIGHTING. Do not neglect the lights. Adequate, flattering lighting is indispensable in a bathroom, because mirrors can be cruel first thing in the morning, and most of us do not look our best fresh out of the shower! Evaluate the natural light conditions of each of your bathrooms, and complement them with plenty of artificial light.

To maximize their flexibility, put bathroom lights on dimmers. You might wish to dim the lights low to mimic candlelight for a tranquil soak in the tub or to softly light the bathroom during a party or to lessen the impact of a night-time trip to the loo. Alternatively, turn the lights up to help with makeup application and close shaves.

We always include an overhead light in the bath (and, separately, in the shower), supplemented by vanity and task lighting. Our favorite solution for evenly balanced vanity lighting is to place a pair of single-arm sconces on either side of the mirror in addition to the overhead ceiling fixture. Discreet overhead recessed lights can also be added.

BATHROOM STORAGE. We abide by the axiom that you can never have too much storage space. Good storage solutions are particularly important in bathrooms where the space is often limited and you have so much to store. Banish clutter by tucking almost everything out of sight. Makeup and blow dryers belong in drawers, unless you are fortunate enough to have a dressing table in the bathroom or bedroom. Our thoughts on bathroom storage are as follows:

Vanity. Although free-standing sinks are attractive and airy, a built-in vanity will conceal the plumbing and offer valuable storage, including a hamper if desired.

Medicine cabinet. Instead of buying a commercially made medicine cabinet, have a carpenter or cabinetmaker build one recessed into the wall over the sink with glass shelves inside and a mirrored front. Around the mirror, which lies flush with the wall, specify a wooden molding to coordinate with the molding in the room.

Shelving. If you do not have a separate linen closet, you can use open shelving to store stacks of towels. Bathroom shelves can display decorative items, but avoid using them to display your toiletries, unless you have no other storage options. If you do need to use the shelves for this kind of storage, accessorize them with a set of colored boxes or deep, woven baskets so that shelves stay organized and attractive. Shelf niches in showers and tubs keep products like shampoo and conditioner neat and close at hand.

Freestanding cabinets. In a spacious bathroom, freestanding pieces of furniture offer unique and beautiful opportunities for storage. We have used étagères, commodes, and armoires to store linens and assorted amenities.

Linen closet. Consider yourself lucky if you have room for a linen closet in the bathroom. A linen closet in an adjacent location will, of course, serve very well.

Decorative Accessories

Linens. Trends in bath linens come and go, so resist the urge to buy this year's hot hue or pattern. Instead, opt for the classics—white toweling and white shower curtains never go out of style. If you simply cannot resist some sort of embellishment, custom embroidery is the elegant answer and a good way to personalize a bathroom. Choose thread colors that match or complement the linens in the bedroom and the tile and stone in your bathroom. If they do not match, they should definitely complement the sheets in the adjacent rooms, or at least all match each other within the bathroom. If you have more than one design, do not use them at the same time. For bathrooms not adjacent to a bedroom, like a powder room, use linen towels with a monogram or another design and simple hemstitching on the bottom edge. These types of towels also make a great house gift for a good friend.

Embroidery can be very simple or very elaborate, as with an inset embroidery panel. Many fine linen stores will do custom work. You may choose from colors or patterns they already have or select a custom-colored thread. Think about the mood you want to evoke when you are

Solutions: Adapting Antique Furniture to the Bathroom

ADD CHARACTER AND INTEREST TO A TINY SPACE LIKE A POWDER ROOM BY INCLUDING SOMETHING PERSONAL AND ANTIQUE. INSTEAD OF USING A PEDESTAL SINK OR CUSTOM CABINET, CONVERT A PIECE OF FURNITURE INTO AN ACTUAL SINK. YOUR CONTRACTOR CAN HELP YOU FIND A SINK AND FAUCET THAT FIT PROPERLY, AND YOU MIGHT WANT TO ATTACH A MARBLE TOP FOR PRACTICALITY.

OPPOSITE: Without a doubt, a marble master bath makes a strong design statement; even the walls in this master bath are covered in marble, for the ultimate in luxury. This bath makes the most of Quetzal green slabs and white Carrara slabs by using the colors to define the architecture of the base molding and the crown. Gilded and crystal hardware and sconces, embroidered towels, artwork, and antiques fill the room with unquestionably formal details. (Barnes, Coy, architects)

choosing colors and patterns. But remember that custom work can be expensive, and in most cases is not returnable. Always request a sample in your colors before you approve an order.

Shower curtains. A custom shower curtain can be made with the same design as the towels. We prefer a nice long curtain that touches the floor. Most ready-made styles are too short to do this—the 72-inch standard size usually does not reach the floor. A linen shop or upholsterer can make a custom size for you using any kind of lightweight, washable cotton or linen you provide. The plastic liner, of course, does not need to touch the floor.

Accessories. These are the wastebaskets, tissue boxes, cups, and so on that can dress your bathrooms in a personal way. Even utilitarian items like these can—and should—be pretty. Although custom and hand-painted styles can be created, there are many attractive ready-made designs available in retail shops that will do very well. Do not just shop in the bathroom aisles. Look elsewhere for woven baskets or tooled leather cans with nail heads for a powder room located next to a paneled study. The point is, accessories offer an irresistible opportunity to add style without spending a fortune. And changing them is the best way to refresh your bathroom without renovating.

Keeping Elevations Up to Date

Once you have selected your bathroom fixtures, fittings, and hardware, send the specifications directly to your architect or contractor so they can be included in the drawings. Clarify, also, who will be purchasing everything. Usually the contractor is the buyer, because he is the only one who knows exactly what he needs, from shower bodies to arcane plumbing devices. Bathroom elevations should also include tile details, such as patterns, moldings, edge and corner tiles, height of tiles, and so on. Tiles should not

Right top:
A small oak cabinet with brass hardware from about 1905 was used to create a sink in this small powder room. Dutch brass sconces with original wall-mounted back plates flank a Tole-framed mirror, which reflects the light from a late-19th-century French brass lantern with its original glass. Wooden wainscoting further enriches this guest bath.

Right bottom:
A 19th-century chest was converted to a vanity, on which Carrara marble protects the wood from splashes. Hand-painted horizontal stripes add a modern rhythm.

Opposite:
In this master bathroom we were striving for "knock your socks off" glamour. There is nothing subtle in this jewel box, whose barrel vault is glazed in platinum leaf that is lightly antiqued so it doesn't look too glitzy. The walls are stenciled in a damask pattern and the floors are white marble with accents of butterscotch onyx.

be ordered unless they work well in the elevations and on the plan. Then the tiles may be carefully counted and ordered on the basis of the drawings. Again, this is a case where the tile installer would most likely be the purchaser because only he knows exactly what is needed.

Closets

The main function of a closet, of course, is to tame your storage. Closets present a unique design challenge, because they may not be rooms per se (although there are some enormous walk-in versions that come close to deserving room status), yet we apply all the same principles used in actual rooms. For every closet, we develop a floor plan, draw elevations, create a cohesive architectural framework, plan a good lighting system, and address assorted basic functions and comfort needs. Closets are extensions of their rooms or of adjacent rooms, so we finish them in a similar aesthetic, with carpet, proper hardware, and paint or wallpaper, to insure that each and every closet is as presentable as the rest of the house.

With appropriate planning, a closet should work just as well years from now as when it is first installed, despite changing fashions and lifestyles.

Assess Your Needs

If you are building a home from scratch or doing a total renovation, lay the groundwork during the floor-plan stage by ascertaining that you have enough closets in the right size and in the right locations. Otherwise, closet planning should take place as early as possible in your decorating process. Whether the carpenter building the cabinetry for the rest of your home is working on your closets, or you are using the services of a closet system shop, you should answer the following questions to assess your closet situation: How many closets do you need? Where is the best location for each closet? Which classifications of closets do you specifically need? (See below for more on closet types.) What kinds of items do you need to store? What type of internal organization do you prefer (drawers, racks, rods, hooks, additional shelving, and so on)?

Creating a Custom Closet

All of our closets are made to order for each client. By using standard ideas and designs and combining them with the specific materials of each job, the results are truly custom closets. Even if

The C&K Way: The Dressing Table

A dressing table, or vanity, provides a welcome place to sit and apply makeup or put on jewelry. The table can be rectangular or kidney-shape and is usually positioned in the dressing room or the bedroom. If you like to apply makeup near a sink, put the dressing table in your bathroom. One seamless way to do so is to lower a section of countertop between two sinks, and add drawers and a kneehole space underneath to accommodate a small stool. It is nice to put a dressing table in front of a window for extra natural light.

If you do not have a tremendous amount to store, a dressing table can be just a simple desk with a pretty chair or stool. If you have a lot of supplies and accoutrements, you might prefer a custom table. We make a wooden table with two pedestals that open up like wings. The entire piece is upholstered. Two upholstered panels are attached to the cabinet doors and open with them to reveal the drawers inside. Make sure you include a glass or mirrored tabletop to avoid staining the fabric.

Whatever set-up you prefer, remember that good lighting is imperative. Give yourself two candlestick lamps flanking a central mirror. You may even find a stand-up mirror with attached candlesticks that light up.

Do You Know? Thinking Outside the (Shoe) Box

Ample shoe storage is requested by nearly all of our clients. We always specify adjustable, horizontal glass shelves that can change with fashion to accommodate tall boots one year and calf-height boots the next. Shoe shelves slanted at an angle are a common feature in many closets for storing and displaying shoes, but they are not adjustable, and they also take up 25 percent more space than horizontal shelves. In most closets, space is at a premium, so when you do the math, horizontal shelves become the obvious choice. And glass is easily cleaned.

Here is another favorite C&K trick: Line up your shoes so that the right and left shoes of each pair alternate toe and heel. This way you can quickly see which heels and toes need freshening, and you will also have a quick reference for heel heights and toe shapes when you are picking out shoes in a rush.

Opposite:
A handwoven rug, soft printed linen, and unlined curtains typify the elegant simplicity of the dressing room/bath of this Nantucket beach house. The C&K design wastebasket was custom-painted to match the walls. (Botticelli and Pohl, architects)

Left:
One of our favorite dressing tables. Hidden beneath the folds of the fabric are rows of drawers for excellent storage. The pair of crystal lamps with smocked lamp shades would provide adequate lighting, but the magnifying mirror with sidelights is a luxurious necessity.

you cannot do this yourself, you should still follow some of our basic rules for storage and try to implement some of our solutions for your own closets.

HANGING. Begin by measuring all of your hanging items and shoes in linear feet, and then allow for at least 25 percent expandability for wardrobes to grow. Specify adjustable hanging bars that can keep up with changes in fashion, because skirt and dress lengths vary from season to season and year to year.

HARDWARE. The finish and style of closet hardware should match the hardware in the room where the closet is located. This includes doorknobs, cabinetry handles, and drawer pulls.

SHELVES. Varied and adjustable shelving can address many storage dilemmas. Cubbies provide small spaces to keep everything from socks and nightgowns to T-shirts and sweaters. We like narrow vertical dividers, like tray storage in a kitchen, to accommodate the many styles, heights, and widths of handbags, from an evening clutch to a knapsack.

Drawers and Dressers

Try combining drawer storage needs where possible to create a built-in dresser within a closet. This setup has several benefits. First, the top surface of the dresser is a good place for storing a daily handbag or sets of keys. Second, drawers should be in graduated sizes to accommodate everything from lingerie, nightgowns, socks, and other hosiery items to tall stacks of T-shirts and the like. There is nothing worse than a drawer that is too deep—things get lost. As a special finishing touch, build and line the top drawer for use as a jewelry box, complete with dividers built in to keep items neatly organized. Other favorite amenities include a mirror over the dresser for a quick check on hair or makeup before going out, a three-way mirror for more in-depth scrutiny, and outlets above the dresser for charging cell phones and PDA devices. If you can, add an extra light just over the mirror. Consider the material of the top surface. Covering it with a luxurious suede or leather surface will act as a noise buffer for tossed keys or protection for jewelry.

Thoughtful Conveniences

Here are a few additional thoughts and suggestions:

*Retractable pulls on vertical dividers allow you to hang garment bags when packing for a trip.

*Hooks on vertical dividers are handy for hanging freshly dry-cleaned or ironed clothing, or items to be tailored.

*To provide a temporary place for folding your clothing, consider installing a tray shelf that pulls out right below the counter.

*If you have valuables on hand, a closet is the perfect place to tuck away a safe. If you think you might like to add a safe to one of your closets, always plan ahead for its installation, because a safe needs special anchoring in the wall.

OPPOSITE:
The typical challenge of a windowless closet is how to keep it light and bright. Try using light paint colors or a light wood, such as this avodire. Lighting also helps, so be sure to include a variety of sources for warmth, just as you would in any room. Here we used suspended light fixtures, a pair of sconces, and recessed lights to illuminate the clothes, which like most men's suits do not have a wide variety of distinguishing color. The top of the built-in chest is elegantly covered in cognac-colored leather, so that keys, watches, and so on do not mark the surface. (John B. Murray, architect)

LEFT:
Glazed and stenciled woodwork articulates the delicacy of this dressing room. (John B. Murray, architect)

CASE STUDY:

This apartment had enough space to "parallel park" his and her bathrooms and dressing rooms. (Elliot Rosenblum, architect)

RIGHT TOP:
His bath is a masculine mix of *verde* antique marble offset by a Calacatta marble on the shower floor, which repeats the off-white of the sink and toilet. The mahogany paneling has a strong rope motif.

RIGHT BOTTOM:
His dressing room continues in French-polished mahogany paneling. The lighting is like a study rather than a closet. Note the decorative overhead gilded bronze dish light and bookcase lights, which shine on the clothes.

In her bath, the green-and-white theme from his bath continues in a paler celadon shade; the floor is Ming green marble, which looks like jade. The freestanding bronze shower projects into the room as a three-dimensional sculptural element. The family of moldings is the same here and in the dressing room, as is the hand-painted Robert Adam–inspired motif of the ceiling.

LEFT BOTTOM:
In her closet, every inch of storage is maximized, with shelving going up to just below the crown molding. The ottoman doubles as a surface for packing and opens to afford additional storage. Decorative pilasters and an acanthus crown add architectural refinement to the space. In a sea of new woodwork, we like to introduce something cozy and antique, such as the Federal chest and gilded mirror, which you can see in the reflection.

Chapter 11: The Collections

YOUR FLOOR PLANS ARE DRAWN, YOUR LIGHTING IS LAYERED, YOUR FURNITURE IS COMFORTABLE AND UPHOLSTERED, AND YOUR CURTAINS CONTROL LIGHT AS THEY ENHANCE THE VIEW. YOUR PALETTE IS EXPRESSED IN YOUR FABRICS AND IN THE TYPES OF WALL COVERINGS YOU HAVE CHOSEN. YOU HAVE CAREFULLY BALANCED FUNCTION WITH AESTHETICS. BUT WHAT WILL SET YOUR HOME APART—WHAT WILL MAKE IT TRULY YOURS—ARE YOUR COLLECTIONS.

COLLECTIONS ARE BOTH THE ICING ON THE CAKE AND ABSOLUTELY ESSENTIAL. A COLLECTION MAY FOCUS ON FURNITURE, RUGS, AND TEXTILES, AND IT MAY ALSO INCLUDE DECORATIVE ACCESSORIES AND WORKS OF FINE ART FOR WALLS, TABLETOPS, AND BOOKSHELVES. THE COMPELLING PART OF DECORATING IS THE COORDINATION AND LAYERING OF YOUR COLLECTIONS WITH YOUR INTERIORS. EVERY AVAILABLE SURFACE OFFERS THE OPPORTUNITY TO ENRICH YOUR INTERIORS WITH THE STORIES THAT YOUR COLLECTIONS HAVE TO TELL ABOUT YOUR CONNECTION TO THE WORLD AROUND YOU.

OPPOSITE:
Twentieth-century paintings serve as an exciting counterpart to 18th- and 19th-century antiques, a look we like to call "young traditional." The art refreshes the antiques, while the traditional pieces give the art a warm and layered backdrop. The painting, by Doris Lee, called *Nude, Red Lattice* (c. 1940), hangs over a mahogany Federal sofa with carved paw feet and a carved three-panel back.

Collecting is the essence of our decorating philosophy. People who collect—or wish to collect—seek out Cullman & Kravis because of our curatorial approach to decorating. We help our clients develop and display collections, steering them toward what is the best of its kind, based on aesthetic and historic significance and what works best in their houses. Eugene Thaw, the eminent art dealer and collector, speaks of collecting as establishing "order." At every step of the way, choices are made and paths taken, creating a logic to every home.

BECOMING A COLLECTOR

Scholars and collectors will categorize pieces according to various aesthetic standards, but all categorization is subject to interpretation and debate. As you collect, recognize that there are different levels of value ascribed to antiques based on their period, rarity, and condition. Over time you will develop an eye for the general classifications of what are considered "good," "better," and "best" in your chosen area of collecting. Our dictum is: "Never rest until the good is better and the better is best." We accept that it is practically impossible to furnish a home completely with "best" examples. But we do try to have one "main event" in every room. By this we mean one superior example of an artwork or an antique that will bring up the tenor of the entire room.

The emotional aspects of collecting can trump whatever technical information you may have. Allow yourself to respond to pieces as you shop. If a piece calls out to you and is hard to resist, give in to your instinct and follow your passion. Or if you come across a piece you love, ask yourself: "What story does the object tell?" And then choose objects that have some common thread and try to weave them together.

"Our challenge is to integrate collections of antiques and works of art with the upholstered furniture, curtains, and rugs to enrich the experience of the room in which they are placed. Our goal is to create a connection between a beloved collection and the design of a room."

RIGHT:
Suburb in Havana (1958, oil on canvas) by Willem de Kooning hangs near a gray sandstone Cambodian sculpture of the goddess Uma from the 12th century.

OPPOSITE:
Create a connection between a beloved collection and the design of your room. This light-filled Long Island dining room was designed with transoms to hold pairs of cow and horse weather vanes, ingeniously allowing you to see them from both sides, as they are meant to be seen. The animal imagery continues with the model of the horse prancing atop the side table and the carving of a dog curled up beneath. (Jacquelyn Robertson, architect)

Do not be afraid to mix things. For example, the seeming mismatch of American folk art and Biedermeier furniture can bring surprisingly attractive results. Usually the styles you respond to have a common ground on some level, even if they are from different periods or cultures. Discovering a shared aesthetic between the elegant and the humble can create a thoughtful harmony throughout a space. If everything were in one style, your home would feel too boring and restrictive. No collection should be so enshrined, nor should a house have an aesthetic so rigorous that you can't accommodate whatever it is you happen to love.

When we talk about collecting, we generally mean the fine arts, such as painting and sculpture, as well as antiques, from fine furniture to decorative objects. As historic pieces, antiques have intrinsic value on many levels, including the fact that they are resalable and they hold their monetary value better than many more common investments.

Antique Furniture

Some people have an unfounded fear of using antiques in their interiors. But after all, if these objects have made it this far in time, chances are that some exposure to your family will not be the end of them. The key to decorating with antiques is to use them, rather than to re-create a historically accurate room that looks and feels like a museum. Antique furniture can include anything from a family heirloom or a gallery piece to an auction house purchase, or if you are very lucky, a thrift-shop gem that has languished until your excellent eye managed to decipher its quality.

Whatever the source, evaluate the piece carefully before you put it into a room. Does it need to be repaired or refinished or reupholstered? Some old wooden pieces may need to be reglued or undergo serious reconstruction. Will the piece serve a function in the room, whether as a desk or table or seating piece? If it is a chair or a settee, is it comfortable to sit in? Is the style or appearance of the object compatible with the

ABOVE LEFT:
High-country furniture, such as the Queen Anne card table and the ladderback chairs, and American folk art, such as the painted horse weather vane and the contemporary hooked rug, live happily with the owner's collection of vintage and contemporary photography by such artists as Duane Michals, Lee Friedlander, Paul Strand, Robert Frank, Charles Sheeler, and Diane Arbus. Hanging a large thematic grouping of framed photographs close together creates density on the wall and makes the collection even more important.

ABOVE RIGHT:
Don't be too rigid about collections. Americana abounds in Ellie's Connecticut house, but her aesthetic is not so strict that she cannot accommodate objects from other cultures. The Napoleon III sideboard was chosen because its paint and carving are reminiscent of American examples.

OPPOSITE:
Sometimes we transform an antique piece or object into a new use. This is a common situation with coffee tables, which did not exist before the 1920s. Our solution is to repurpose historical pieces, such as the blanket chest shown here, which now serves as a coffee table.

other pieces in the room? Your placement of the piece will depend on your answers to these questions. But the most important question really is: Do you love the object? If you do, you will find a way to make it work in the room.

Second Period and Antique Reproductions

Despite our passion for antiques, sometimes we are obliged to use reproductions because we cannot find the desired form or because the form is prohibitively expensive. In this scenario, our first instinct is to look for what are called "second period" antiques—nineteenth-century copies of eighteenth-century forms, or twentieth-century copies of nineteenth-century forms. A period reproduction from the 1920s or the 1930s at least has some age on it, unlike a brand-new piece, and thus, will have a resale value at auction. If our search proves futile, we might create a reproduction of what we are looking for. We try not to buy commercial reproductions for our clients. Instead, we create one-of-a-kind, custom reproductions using talented craftspeople.

Another situation we often face is the need to add dining chairs to complete an existing set. For example, if we have a set of eight chairs and we want twelve, we will make four custom reproduction chairs to match and have the cabinetmaker's name and the date marked on the underside of the chair so there is no confusion in years to come if the set is resold.

For budget purposes, we will sometimes buy one period mirror or one period console and have them replicated. The cost of each "pair" is a fraction of an original pair of antiques, but of course less valuable at resale.

Decorative Arts

The term "decorative arts" includes more than furniture. It encompasses objects such as pottery and porcelain, glass, silver, brass, and textiles, which can be further classified by period, maker, color, and pattern. Or, it might be a collection of a variety of objects reflecting a particular style, such as folk art, or a theme such as nautical, or an era such as Art Deco, or even a geographical location such as Asia.

Whatever your interest, keep in mind that every room needs significant signature pieces as well as filler pieces to help it feel complete. Signature pieces are those that define a room—they make a statement and elevate the interior with their presence. A few signature pieces should anchor your collections, your rooms, and your home.

ANTIQUE MIRRORS. If you find an antique mirror with a great frame, but you do not like the actual mirror glass—perhaps it has darkened or become spotted to the point where it no longer reflects well—you need not replace or attempt to repair it. If the mirror is going to be used simply as a decorative object, we would recommend leaving it alone, especially if the frame and mirror are valuable. Remember, the less an antique object is interfered with, the better.

However, if you really want to use the mirror, you can replace the reflective glass. Be sure to save the old mirror, the backing, and the old nails in the event you decide to resell the mirror one day. You can even attach the old mirror to the back of the frame so that it will not be misplaced or damaged. If the mirror is elaborately shaped, beveled, or otherwise hard to match, it may be possible to resilver the back of the mirror. Obviously, resilvering does change the integrity of the original mirror and can be costly. You should go this route only if you are not worried about the resale value of the original piece.

OPPOSITE:
What could be more different than a traditional interior with a Queen Anne wing chair covered in damask, polychrome Delft garniture, and brass accessories, along with a photograph of Chuck Close with a cigarette dangling from his lips? We call the style of this living room in Greenwich, Connecticut, "Opposites Attract." The contrast of the chair and the photography—what we call the "curve ball"—liberates the room from being simply functional and well decorated to being unforgettable.

LEFT:
This formal entry references themes that are repeated throughout the apartment, including a fairly monochromatic palette, 19th-century antiques, and a sprinkling of Asian artifacts, which reflect the owner's five-year stay in the Far East. The graceful sweep of the entry staircase is enhanced by the bronze hand balustrade. (John B. Murray, architect)

Graniteware was the disposable dishware of the 19th century and is still relatively inexpensive. The abstract patterns of the swirling designs are made from baked enamel on metal and evoke the gestural swirl of contemporary abstract painting. Sometimes it makes a better statement to group accessories like these rather then to spread them around evenly.

ABOVE RIGHT:
Blue-and-white spongeware, a type of American folk pottery of the 19th century, is used in counterpoint to polychrome French Quimper ware from the early 20th century. Brass candlesticks add shine and the miniature stars add whimsy. The star on the lower right is inscribed "for a good girl" and was a gift to Ellie.

RIGHT:
Take advantage of every possible opportunity to display your collections. Window niches in a side entry are the perfect spot for a group of glass bottles.

On the other hand, you may find a new or vintage mirror that you wish to age. A good mirror or glass supplier can darken or spot the new piece of mirror to give it an antique look, while still allowing you to be able to see your reflection clearly.

Fine Art

Art is very personal. There is no more powerful way to express one's personality than by hanging objects on the wall. Whether you have oil paintings, drawings, prints, or photographs, something of visual interest on the walls always enhances the character of a room.

One of the biggest decisions is whether you want your art collection to include traditional easel paintings or more contemporary works. Not surprisingly, this decision will have an impact on the floor plan by posing questions such as: Should the sofas be on the wall or off the wall? What type of framing, pedestals, or spacing will the art pieces require? How will they be lit? As you design the floor plans, think about where you want to put works of art in each room. Photograph each piece digitally and then make a small-scale copy to lay onto the elevation drawings to see how it will look. For a client with a large collection, we try to keep track of where everything will go. If you do not yet own works of art but plan to, draw in the optimal sizes on each wall so that you know what you are looking for.

FRAMES. In addition to considering the frame's relationship to the art itself, your choice should also take its cues from your furnishings and architecture. For example, a room with minimal moldings should not have elaborately gilded frames or rich woods unless you are looking for this contrast.

LEFT:
Because the 19th-century barley box was not a precious antique, we added a layer of whitewash to refresh the finish and to make it suitable for use as a side table. Hanging on the wall above are three C-prints from the Gouville series by artist Gotz Diergarten.

Scale is another issue in frame selection. How does your frame compare to the size of the art? To the scale of your room? To the scale of other art works in the room? Pay attention to proportions. A room with low ceilings should not have very large frames unless you wish to play with scale by using oversize frames to trick the eye. Before you make a decision, try a frame on your wall first to make sure that it works. Or use a computer to superimpose frames over digital images of the art and make your decision that way.

You may decide to select the look and materials of your frame based on the location of your house. A beach house would call for simpler frames in light woods, whereas a city residence might require a stronger-looking frame, perhaps gilded or in a heavier wood. Whether you opt for light or dark, rustic or polished, avoid a commercial or "hotel" look by using several different materials and styles of frames.

You can always choose a tasteful "non-denominational" frame, as opposed to a "statement" frame. Your living space may change, or the usage of the same rooms could change. But if a frame has no dominating aesthetic style, that is one less thing to worry about when you are moving art around. That way, also, the focus is on the art. Remember, the purpose of a frame is to *frame*, not to overpower the contents. A frame that is neutral in its aesthetic connotations can be integrated into a variety of interiors.

The C&K Way: Refinishing Antiques

IF YOU ARE CONCERNED ABOUT THE CONDITION OF A PIECE OF ANTIQUE FURNITURE OR WISH TO ALTER IT FOR SOME REASON, THERE ARE SEVERAL WAYS OF "FIXING" IT. BUT IF YOU WANT TO CHANGE SOMETHING ABOUT AN OBJECT, BE SURE TO DO YOUR RESEARCH FIRST, BECAUSE YOUR DECISIONS CAN HAVE IRREVERSIBLE IMPLICATIONS ON THE VALUE OF THE PIECE. REFINISHING CERTAIN ANTIQUE PIECES MAY ACTUALLY DETRACT FROM THEIR VALUE. AS IN MANY AREAS OF COLLECTING, SUCH AS ARTS AND CRAFTS FURNITURE, ORIGINAL CONDITION IS KEY. IF YOU ARE UNSURE, OUR BEST ADVICE IS TO HAVE THE OBJECT EVALUATED BY A KNOWLEDGEABLE PERSON, SUCH AS YOUR ANTIQUE-FURNITURE DEALER OR THE EXPERT AT AN AUCTION HOUSE OR A MUSEUM CURATOR.

RIGHT TOP:
The Damien Hirst butterfly painting with its electric blue ground is the centerpiece of a contemporary-art collector's living room that is primarily beige, tan, and blue.

RIGHT BOTTOM:
A gouache by Willem de Kooning, c. 1965, is framed in a traditional manner, which is in keeping with the décor of the home.

OPPOSITE:
Often the whole is greater than the sum of its parts. This set of Joseph Albers prints is framed with identical white mats and frames, which allows them to be grouped together as a single work of art. Hanging on the wall behind the sofa is the complete portfolio of silk screens from *Homage to the Square: Edition Keller* (1970) by Albers.

OPPOSITE:
Sometimes it is necessary to commission artwork for a special project. This entrance hall in South Carolina was three stories high, so we commissioned artist Sarah Hinckley to paint a series of six abstract canvases that would work well together in the space. The paintings also evoke the quality of the local beach light, the far horizon, and the endless shoreline that surrounds the home.

ABOVE:
This flying-geese quilt is hung on the wall like a painting, but textiles, like paper, are very fragile and should not be hung in direct light. Quilts were originally considered only as utilitarian objects— bedcovers—until pioneer collectors of folk art in the 1920s and 1930s recognized them as works of art because of their graphic and original designs.

BOOKCASES. Books are a collectible like any other object, and they should be displayed and assembled with care. More than just a storage place for your volumes, bookcases can be a display space to flaunt your collections and transform a room from everyday to extraordinary. But bookshelves need to be carefully designed. Adding air space is the first requirement: no shelf should be more than two-thirds to three-quarters full of books. It is also a good idea to introduce objects that are not books, such as framed photos or small, flat artworks, and then three-dimensional objects, such as porcelain or sculptures. Finally, look at each shelf individually and then at the entire wall to find a pleasing composition. You should aim to create some sort of a rhythm or checkerboard as a feast for the eye.

RIGHT:
A collection can be closely related or just a random gathering of pieces tethered to each other by the rules of your own taste. In this bookcase, sandstone sculptures from India contrast with blue-and-white tobacco jars, covered vases, plates, a flat-screen television, and, of course, books. Note the diagonal composition of the object families and the careful inclusion of openness, or air space, around everything. The painted fretwork grille on the shelf and the open grilles on the lower cabinets conceal speakers, and the metal grilles integrated into the upper frieze are for air supply.

LEFT TOP:
Although walls of books are often the best decoration of all, the bookshelves in this folk art collector's country home include a mix of sculptural objects. The slight surfeit of shelf space allows each component to harmonize with the others.

LEFT BOTTOM:
The display of pottery in this English pine dresser and rack from the late 18th century is as carefully thought through as any bookcase. The collection includes 19th-century soft paste pottery in pale creams, browns, and greens, all offset by the vivid green Bristol wine glasses and majolica leaf dishes.

RIGHT TOP:
Display only the things that you love. Pieces that have meaning and history are always better than fakes and clutter. This avodire-wood bookcase includes mementos of travels to the Far East. A collection of Chinese ceremonial jades in subtle shades of green, called "Bi" from the Neolithic period, c. 3500–2500 B.C., are mounted on iron bases and displayed along with Japanese 18th-century sliding panels.

TABLETOPS. Every tabletop presents the same considerations as the floor plan of a room. The elements can be studied both in plan and in elevation for visual harmony so that the tabletop creates a cosmos of form, material, and color.

Most people make the mistake of organizing their tabletops in what we call "altar style." By this we mean a tabletop where a pair of objects, often lamps, flanks another pair and focuses on a central object. But this kind of design is rigid and two-dimensional. Instead, aim for asymmetry in the grouping and a mix of tall and short, round and rectilinear, three-dimensional and flat pieces.

Tabletops, like bookcases, must be arranged and organized with thought. A room is not really complete until all the surfaces achieve their maximum potential. Relate to the principles of Japanese flower arranging in which there are three elements—foreground, middle ground, and background—and only one object in the group is dominant. Be careful, however. Lamps tend to dominate any table, so make sure they do not.

If you have an extensive art collection, or intend to build one, it is helpful to hire an art consultant to help you address any special needs for your collection. Based on the art, you may have to install some sort of controls for climate and light, as well as additional security. Because these elements can affect your home design, it is best to address this while you are still working with your architect or contractor on your floor plans. You may also want to seek the advice of a conservator or art restorer to assess the condition of your art. Works on paper, for example, must not remain on permanent display because they will suffer deterioration from light if exposed for more than a few months. Frames, mats, glass, and other containers for works of art should be reviewed by an expert for quality of materials.

RIGHT TOP:
Sometimes the inspiration for a tabletop is thematic. From the peacock weather vane to the tramp-art box, this gathering of art and objects is all about American folk art.

RIGHT BOTTOM:
The tabletop in this library is a mini art-history lesson about Cubism, which traces some of its roots to African art. The inspiration for the 1912 Juan Gris self-portrait that hangs on the wall is seen in the photograph of an African mask by Charles Sheeler, an early American Modernist.

ABOVE:
This symmetrical arrangement is anything but static. The 15th-century Tibetan manuscript cover and the 19th-century Anglo-Indian quill box are effectively juxtaposed with a 1972 Willem de Kooning painting, which is flanked by four Philip Guston drawings from 1952.

CASE STUDY:

This is our final case study, the entry to Ellie's apartment. Look at this picture and see how it illuminates everything that we have shared with you in the course of this book. Consider the harmony between the architectural envelope, the lighting, the hard and soft materials, and the decorations. Yet what makes this space personal and meaningful are the collections and how they connect the site to Ellie herself. Her passion for American art is seen in the iconographic still life by William Michael Harnett and her love of Asian art in the set of nineteenth-century China trade paintings. The pattern of the faux-painted floor was based on an inlaid marquetry floor that she saw in Saint Petersburg on a trip to Russia, while her admiration for neoclassicism is reflected in the Swedish mahogany commode and the American Empire center table. A pair of modern Maison Jansen chairs, upholstered in bright blue fabric, adds a welcome pop of color.

We hope this image will set you out on your own decorating journey— in the Cullman & Kravis way, of course. By paying close attention to the lessons you've learned from this book and to your personal tastes and interests, you can create your own environment, one that is both comfortable and inspiring, a shelter for your soul.

Setting Up Your Project Book

To be a decorator, you need to be incredibly organized and detail oriented. Most of our day is not spent shopping for fabrics and objects, as one might expect. We are usually researching ideas, making phone calls, keeping records, and filing paperwork.

In order to stay organized and to work efficiently, we create project books, which serve as an evolving record of all our plans and decisions. These books are revised and referred to again and again throughout the duration of the project.

We recommend that you create several books (we use three-hole binders) for each project, with tabs for every room—living room, dining room, hallway, entrance, kitchen, master bath, downstairs bath, closets, and so on.

The first binder, which we call a "cut-sheet book," contains floor plans, elevations, and material samples, such as fabric and paint swatches, organized by room. Bulkier items, such as samples of wood, stone, tiles, or hardware, can be marked with the name of the room and kept in a big clear plastic box, which we call a "sample box," for easy handling and quick reference.

The second binder, also arranged by room, is where we file copies of all paperwork—memos, estimates, purchase orders, invoices, shipping bills, and other supplier information—for every item purchased. Be sure to include notes on telephone conversations, measurements and specifications, cost estimates from members of your design team (architect, decorator, contractor, etc.) and their contact information. You may even wish to include photocopies of calendar pages to stay on top of work schedules and deliveries.

Finally, we create an inventory book, which consists of photographs and a list of all antiques and art that have been purchased for the project. This book is also organized by room. A copy of the inventory book makes an excellent record for insurance purposes.

For very large projects, we make a comprehensive book that contains pictures of all items in storage, and we sometimes set up a separate lighting book with pictures and dimensions of all lights in the house.

Every time you address a new topic in the chapters of this book, update the relevant sections in your project book. Below are some tips for updating and maintaining your project books by chapter.

Chapter 2: The Floor Plan

Floor plans are an integral part of your project book, and you should maintain the most up-to-date version for each room. Insert the individual room plans into plastic sleeves and put them at the beginning of each relevant room section. As your designs progress, you can color in the plan as you choose rugs, fabrics, paint colors, and so on. The plan essentially becomes a map representing your new room. You may find it helpful to number each of the items on the plan for easier reference to other sections. These plans can be popped out of the binder at any time and taken along on shopping trips so you will always know the dimensions of items you are looking for.

Chapter 3: The Hardscape

Make notes of all your stone and wood choices, including colors and stains. If possible, collect actual samples of each material and mark them with numbers that refer to descriptions in your cut-sheet book.

Take or find photographs of important architectural elements in each room, such as doors, windows, or fireplace mantels, as well as drawings of molding options or custom floor patterns.

Ask your architect or contractor to produce detailed elevations for such details as paneling, wainscoting, chair rails, and so on.

Don't forget to photograph and file all information on hardware.

Chapter 4: The Lighting

Add lighting plans for each room to your cut-sheet binder. Also include photographs or line drawings, as well as the dimensions of the lights you choose for every room. You may wish to make a master list of the lights you plan to purchase, so that nothing gets left out; be sure to include desired sizes, locations, and wattage.

Include purchase orders of all lighting fixtures in your paperwork binder.

Chapter 5: The Soft Materials

Thanks to the decisions you have made in this chapter, you will start to see your rooms come to life with color and pattern in your project books. Be sure to include photographs of any antique rugs you are planning to purchase or ones that you already own. If you are going to have custom rugs made, add small clippings of the yarns and a drawing of the pattern to the cut-sheet book.

Make a card that shows the fabric scheme for each room, complete with swatches. You can cut same-size swatches of fabric with pinking shears, label them, and attach them to the cards. Or you can simply clip them all together by room or put them in plastic sleeve pockets.

Don't forget to keep receipts and invoices of all purchases in your paperwork binder. Maintain a calendar indicating lead times and delivery dates for your rugs and fabrics. It is extremely important to create a paper trail when you are decorating. We always order cuttings for approval (CFA) because dye lots of fabrics often fail to match the sample in the showroom. When you approve your CFA, you must keep the sample with a copy of the order. We also record the name of the person we spoke to at the fabric house, as well as the date on which we approved the sample. Keep track of estimates to confirm you have been billed the correct price when the item is delivered.

Chapter 6: The Upholstery

On the floor plans, draw, or have a professional draw, scale images of the furniture forms you have selected. Indicate your upholstery selections for each piece, using colored pencils in appropriate colors for easy visual reference, or label which fabrics will appear on the different pieces. For each piece of furniture, attach a photograph of the piece and swatches of final fabrics and trims, as well as dimensions. Continue to review these visuals throughout the process to be sure you have not repeated any one form or fabric too much.

Collect any new purchase orders and record all details for each piece, such as whether the fabric and trim has been received by the upholsterer.

Chapter 7: The Windows

For each room section, include photographs or line drawings of your curtain designs, to which you can add swatches of fabrics and trims and selected hardware. Make a note of dimensions for each window.

Collect purchase orders for both curtains and hardware, and keep track of delivery dates.

Chapter 8: Adding Color

Include a small paint chip or decorative paint sample with your fabrics and floor plans in your cut-sheet book. Don't forget to include wallpaper and wall upholstery fabrics if you're using them. By the time you get to the painting stage, your cut-sheet workbook should be almost complete and can provide you with an overview of the entire project.

Stain samples for floors, cabinetry, and woodwork will also go into this section, or into your sample box.

Chapter 9: The Kitchen

Collect photographs and measurements of all kitchen appliances and light fixtures in your cut-sheet binder. Attach swatches of any new paint colors or materials for any kitchen chair pads, window coverings, curtains, linens, and so on.

If you have a small sample of your flooring or countertop material, put it in the sample box.

Include photographs of all your entertaining accessories: glasses, flatware, china, linens, and so on. It is good to have these for reference when you are out shopping and see some new pieces you might like to add.

Chapter 10: Bathrooms and Closets

Keep colors swatches for paints, tile samples, and pieces of stones in your sample box or book, and update your copy of the elevation drawings with lighting details, including fixtures. Also add photographs or line drawings of faucets and other fittings, as well as of any freestanding furniture pieces. If you have ordered custom linens, or if you have commissioned custom embroidery, include swatches of thread colors from towels and line drawings or photocopies of embroidery patterns. Collect and file all purchase orders for custom linens.

Chapter 11: The Collections

Begin another binder or a file in your paperwork binder to document your antiques and other valuables for insurance purposes. Organize the pieces by room, list each item, and provide bills, estimates, purchase orders, any authentication papers where applicable (such as when recording an antique chair), and photographs. Depending on the size of the project, this could grow into two or more binders.

Bibliography

Banks-Pye, Roger. *Colefax and Fowler: Interior Inspirations.* London: Ryland Peters & Small, 1997

Clifton-Mogg, Caroline, and Melanie Paine. *The Art and Technique of Decorating with Fabric.* New York: Prentice Hall Press, 1988

———. *Curtains, a Design Source Book.* London: Ryland Peters & Small, 1997

Cornforth, John. *The Inspiration of the Past.* Middlesex, U.K.: Viking, in association with *Country Life*, 1985

De Bonneville, Françoise. *The Book of the Bath.* New York: Rizzoli, 1997

Gray, Susan. *Designers on Designers: The Inspiration behind Great Interiors.* New York: McGraw-Hill, 2004

Hampton, Mark. *Legendary Decorations of the Twentieth Century.* New York: Doubleday, 1992

———. *On Decorating.* New York: Random House, 1989

Hayward, Helena. *World Furniture, an Illustrated History from Earliest Times.* New York: Crescent Books, 1965

Hoppen, Stephanie. *The New Curtain Book: Master Classes with Today's Top Designers.* New York: Bulfinch Press, 2003

———. *Perfect Neutrals, Color You Can Live With.* New York: Watson-Guptill, 2006

Jackman, Dianne R.,. and Mary K. Dixon. *Guide to Textiles for Interior Designers.* Canada: Peguis Publishers, 1983

Juracek, Judy A. *Surfaces.* New York and London: W. W. Norton, 1996

Kaufman, Donald, and Taffy Dahl. *Color and Light: Luminous Atmospheres for Painted Rooms.* New York: Clarkson Potter, 1999

Kaufman, Donald, and Taffy Dahl. *Color: Natural Palettes for Painted Rooms.* New York: Clarkson Potter, 1992

Madden, Chris Casson. *Kitchens: Information and Inspirations for Managing Kitchens, the Heart of the Home.* New York: Clarkson Potter, 1993

McCloud, Kevin. *Choosing Colors: An Expert Choice of the Best Colors to Use in Your Home.* New York: Watson-Guptill, 2003

McCorquodale, Charles. *The History of the Interior.* New York: Vendome Press, 1983

Metcalf, Pauline C. *Ogden Codman and the Decoration of Houses.* Boston: Boston Athenaeum, 1988

Morley, John. *The History of Furniture, Twenty-Five Centuries of Style and Design in the Western Tradition.* New York: Bulfinch Press, 1999

Nemati, Parviz. *The Splendor of Antique Rugs and Tapestries.* New York: Rizzoli, 2001

Rompilla, Ethel. *Color for Interior Design.* New York: Harry N. Abrams, 2005

Walker, C. Howard. *Theory of Mouldings.* New York: W. W. Norton, 2007

Wilhide, Elizabeth. *The Flooring Book: The Essential Source Book for Planning, Selecting, and Restoring Floors.* London: Ryland Peters & Small, 1997

Wrey, Lady Caroline. *The Complete Book of Curtains and Drapes.* Woodstock N.Y.: Overlook Press, 1991

Index

Page numbers in italics refer to illustrations

Acknowledgments

We owe special thanks to a great many people:

Paige Rense, for her loyal and long-standing support of our work.

Durston Saylor, whose genius translated our three-dimensional spaces into truly magical photographs.

The many other talented photographers who contributed to the additional spectacular images you see in our book: Peter Aaron, Michael Arnaud, Bruce Buck, Billy Cunningham, Scott Francis, Robert Gregg, Sam Grey, Keith Scott Morton, Michael Mundy, and Peter Peirce.

Our clients, who have been a constant inspiration, always taking us to new places, both literally and figuratively.

Our colleagues, who from the early days have helped to shape the "C&K way."

Our current staff: Lee Cavanaugh, Allison Davis, Cristin deVeer, Lizzy Dexter, Sandra Effron, Ali Epstein, Cori Fernandez, Jenny Fischbach, Kim Kaczmarek, Melissa Koch, Amanda Lowenthal, Alyssa Miller; Elena Philips, Sarah Ramsey, Claire Ratliff, Isabel Rutherfoord, and our controller Ellen Chopay, CPA.

Our "alums": Cory Appleman, Penny Ashford, Allison Babcock, Sheryl Bucci, Leigh Chiu, Lisa Davidson, Jennifer Flanders, Lisa Goodwyn, Nicolette Horn, Kelley Johnson, Liz Kohn, Amanda Reynal, and Arden Stephenson.

The many artists, artisans, contractors, vendors, and antique dealers who have realized our projects with grace and ease: We salute you. Without your incredible expertise and immeasurable skills, our work would be impossible.

Extra special thanks to Lindsay Allen, Stephen Anderson, Joe Beam, Tony and Natalie Candela, Joe Calagna and Izzy Jimenez, Jimmy and Barbara Cogema, Janet Golinski and Faith Strashun, Peter Cosola,

Donna Danicic, Virginia DiSciasio, Elizabeth Eakins, Miriam Ellner, Chris Isles and Ed Rollins, Nick Johnson, Mark Martinez, Gregory Newham, Mike Pell, Eli Rios, Ernie Smith and Evelyn Crescimanni, Joe Stegmeyer, Ruben Teles and James Adams, Allen Thorpe, Mark Uriu, Gabe Velasquez, Dorothy Wako, Josh Weiner, Steve Williams, and our trusted MZ movers, under Michael Zreick's leadership.

The architects, who have been such valued and creative partners: John B. Murray, Charlotte Worthy, William Mincey and Jeff Wooley—with whom we have had the longest collaboration. In addition, Marc Appleton, Rob Barnes and Chris Coy, Rink Dupont, Mark Finlay, Ann Fairfax and Richard Sammons, Ira Grandberg, Allan Greenberg, Ed Hollander and Maryann Connolly, Lyman Perry, Gordon Pierce, Ray Pohl and Lisa Botticelli, Andrew Pollock, Jacquelyn Robertson, Elliot Rosenblum, Oscar Shamamian and Mark Ferguson, Stephen Miller Siegel, Jeffrey Smith, Robert A.M. Stern, John Tackett, and Reginald Thomas. Thanks to Francesca Bettridge for her lighting designs and to Joel Pidel for his drawings.

The writers who have so ably captured the spirit of our work in their words: Steven M. L. Aronson, Gerald Clarke, Stephen Drucker, Jamee Gregory, Lee Goff, Kira Wilson Gould, Peter Haldeman, Nicholas von Hoffman, Jonathan Kandell, Chris Casson Madden, Wendy Moonan, Ann Sample, Suzanne Slesin, Suzanne Stephens, Jean Strouse, and Annette Tapert.

Thanks are due to Eric Himmel, editor in chief of Harry N. Abrams, without whose support this book would not have come to pass. Great appreciation as well goes to Barbara Burn, our editor, and Robert McKee, our book designer; their insight and guidance were invaluable.

We also want to acknowledge Karen Gantz and Jennifer Cegielski, who were with us from the beginning of this journey.

And of course, thanks to those on the "home front"—Edgar Cullman Jr. and Robert Pruzan; Trip, Sam, and Georgina Cullman; Alison and Ben Pruzan, also to Tracey's mom, Ellie Winn, and to Ana Gimenez.

Editor: Barbara Burn
Designer: Robert McKee
Production Manager: Jules Thomson

Page 2: Ellie's dining room in Manhattan with
18th-century Chinese wallpaper.

Page 3: Ellie's living room in Manhattan with the
first piece of art she ever purchased: a 17th-century
Japanese Tosa-school screen with a view of Kyoto.

Library of Congress Cataloging-in-Publication Data

Cullman, Elissa.
  Decorating master class / by Elissa Cullman and
Tracey Pruzan ;
photographs by Durston Saylor.
    p. cm.
  ISBN 978-0-8109-9390-7
1. Interior decoration. 2. Cullman & Kravis (Firm)
I. Pruzan, Tracey.
II. Title.

  NK2115.C973 2008
  747—dc22
                            2007046003.
ISBN 978-0-8109-9390-7

Copyright © 2008 Elissa Cullman and Tracey Pruzan

Printed and bound in China

10 9 8 7 6 5 4 3

Abrams books are available at special discounts when
purchased in quantity for premiums and promotions
as well as fundraising or educational use. Special edi-
tions can also be created to specification. For details,
contact specialmarkets@hnabooks.com or the address
below.

HNA ▮▮▮▮▮
harry n. abrams, inc.
a subsidiary of La Martinière Groupe

115 West 18th Street
New York, NY 10011
www.abramsbooks.com

Photo Credits

All photographs in this book were taken by Durston
Saylor for Cullman & Kravis, except as noted below:

Photographs by Durston Saylor for *Architectural
Digest*. Copyright © 1995 Condé Nast Publications,
pages 2, 4, 73, 117, 190; © 1997, pages 56 (bottom),
184; © 1998, pages 41, 42, 111, 149; © 1999, page
102; © 2000, page 174 (bottom); © 2002, pages 86,
88, 106, 200; © 2003, pages 15, 28 (top), 112; © 2004,
page 70; © 2005, pages 51, 166 (top), 174 (top), 203; ©
2006, pages 2, 32, 61, 69, 71, 78 (bottom, 91, 107, 135,
139, 144–45, 148, 189, 214–15 © 2007, page 23. Reprinted by permission. All rights reserved.

Photographs on pages 7, 12, 16, 125 by Peter Aaron
for *Architectural Digest*. Copyright © 2003 Condé
Nast Publications. Reprinted by permission. All rights
reserved.

Photographs on pages 24–25, 115, 141, 199, 209 by
Scott Frances for *Architectural Digest*. Copyright ©
2007 Condé Nast Publications. Reprinted by permission. All rights reserved.

Photograph on pages 33, 57, 123 (below left), 132, 147,
171 by Michel Arnaud. Copyright © Harpo, Inc
2006. All rights reserved.

Bruce Buck: page 49; Mark Ferry: page 13; Sam Gray:
pages 78, 167; Robert Gregg: pages 19, 31, 58 (top
right), 168 (top); Keith Scott Morton: pages 27, 36
(above right), 46, 74, 114, 121, 140, 186, 188 (top
right); Michael Mundy: pages 8, 9, 10, 11.